POETRY COMES OUT OF MY MOUTH

Selected Poems

Mario Santiago Papasquiaro

Translated by

Arturo Mantecón

Artwork by

Maceo Montoya

Poetry Comes Out of My Mouth
an English translation of Selected Poems
by Mario Santiago Papasquiaro
Translated by Arturo Mantecón
With original art by Maceo Montoya

Printed in the U.S.A.
First Printing
10 9 8 7 6 5 4 3 2 1   18 19 20 21 22 23

Book and Cover design: Bill Lavender
Cover Art: Maceo Montoya

Library of Congress Control Number: 2018934288
Papasquiaro, Mario Santiago
Poetry Comes out of My Mouth / Mario Santiago Papasquiaro
Introduction by Ilan Stavans
with Arturo Mantecón, translator
and Maceo Montoya, illustrator;
p. cm.
ISBN: 978-1-944884-40-6 (pbk.)

DIÁLOGOS BOOKS
DIALOGOSBOOKS.COM

Acknowledgements

Diálogos Books offers grateful acknowledgement to the following for permission to publish these poems.
To Fondo de Cultura Económica for permission to use the following from *Jeta de santo* (Antología poética, 1974-1997). All poems from *Jeta de Santo* are copyright © 2008, by:
Fondo de Cultura Económica.
Todos los derechos reservados. Ciudad de México.
Esta edición consta de 500 ejemplares.

Cabaret Voltaire
Bataille reencarnado
Correspondencia infra
Abisinia's shock
Vision en sinaí
Vas a morir como 1 ganglio de luz que se ha
    vuelto loco
Vas a morir/ entre silencios cojos
Después del electroshock la bartolina
Monte de Venus
Sinaí
Tierra colorada
Contrarretablo
José Revueltas / el día de su expulsión de la
    liga leninista espartaco
La poesía sale de mi boca…
William Shakespeare llega a chilpancingo
Canción implacable
Jeta de santo
Cempazúchitl púrpura
Consejos de 1 discípulo de Marx a 1 fanático
    de Heidegger
Retrato de memoria de mi padre Jack Kerouac/
    desde esta estación del universo
El loco de Pound ha venido a verme
Carta abierta Kenneth Rexroth
Retrato dibujado de memoria en alguna
    estación del universo
En busca del ave del paraíso
Única sangre
¡Salud!
Confesión de Juan Diego
La última balada del sol
Mallarmé asaltado
¿A 10.000 Millones de años luz?
Daría todo todo todo
Comencemos / con las arboledas de la sangre
Desahogo

Virgen & mártir del rock & roll
Para Nuestra Señora de Guadalumpen
Alias el Socrates
Sexus
Tributo a John Coltrane: pelea a 1 solo round
    con Jack Johnson
Visiones de la rue morgue
Nosotros/ que por doquiera buscamos la
    aventura
Arponeada la luna
Ya lejos de la carretera
Saliva de San Juan Autista
Las memorias de Peter Pan
Para Patricia/ sierra-tortuga/ antisiquiatra-
    mazateca/ maestra-letra de corrido/ amiga-
    cosquilla/ loca desigual & combinada/
    mujer-latidos de hongo/ patafísica con
    plumas/ (la otra noche te soñé con plumas/
    patíbulo al alba)
Forjando 1 chaparrito flautín de rhythm &
    blues
Escudo de crin : brazos de cristal

To Mowgli Zendejas for permission to re-publish the following from *Aullido de cisne* (Al Este del Paraiso).
Carte d'identité
San Juan de la Cruz le da 1 aventón a Neal
    Cassady /en la frontera entre el mito & el
    sueño/
Adolescencia bisiesta
Hijos del Rey Lopitos
Desespejo
Quién sino tú
Azorado el rayo
Ecce homo
Sin embargo sobrevuelo como 1 dinastía de
    soles
Leopoldo María

To Editorial Almadia for permission to re-publish three poems from *Arte & Basura*:
Demasiado viejo para seguir rocanroleando,
    demasiado joven para morir
Tuve un sueño
3 segundos sobrio & enloquezco

Also by Mario Santiago Papasquiaro

Beso eterno, Mexico City: Al Este del Paraiso, 1995.

Aullido de cisne, Mexico City: Al Este de Paraiso, 1996.

Jeta de santo, Poetry Anthology (1974-1977), Compiled by Rebeca López and Mario Raúl Guzmán, Mexico City: Fondo de Cultura Económica, 2008.

Respiración del laberinto, Mexico City: Ediciones la Cartonera, 2008.

Arte & basura, Selection and Prologue by Luis Felipe Fabre, Oaxaca: Almadia, 2012.

Advice from 1 Disciple of Marx to 1 Heidegger Fanatic, Translated by Cole Heinowitz and Alexis Graham, Seattle and New York: Wave Books, 2013.

Índice

Contents

Paintings by Maceo Montoya

Translator's Note

Transforming the work of Mario Santiago Papasquiaro (the nom de plume et guerre of José Alfredo Zendejas) into English was not an easy task for this translator. Rewarding, yes, and abundantly so. There is much that is stunning in his lines and much that is beautifully mysterious in the quiet that surrounds the clash of his colliding words. But the gold of his poetry is embedded in a great deal of mud-like incomprehensibility. Mario Santiago is for the treasure hunter. Expect some hard work. Expect some rewards.

Complicating the chore of translation is Mario Santiago's frequent use of Mexican slang. Though I am a Chicano ("Pocho" is more accurate.) and am quite familiar with some of the colloquialisms, a lot of them threw me for a loss, and I had to resort to a friend more conversant than I am with Mexican—especially Chilango—argot.

The poetry abounds with references to Mexican popular culture—singers, movie stars, left wing political figures, dedications to friends, heroes, and muses. Juan Felipe Fabre somewhere writes that Mario Santiago had much of the "fan" about him. He dropped the names of many of the writers and musicians that influenced him: Rimbaud, The Doors, Artaud, Pound, Beckett, Bataille, Mallarmé, Burroughs, Panero, Kerouac, Ginsberg, Cassady, Rexroth, Lou Reed, Brautigan, Shakespeare, and on and on.

He frequently uses words derived from Nahuatl, the pre-Columbian language of the Mexica and several other indigenous nations, and these words, for the most part, I chose not to translate. I kept them intact for their beauty and their tremendous savor.

As a result, because of so many recondite references to people, places, and things, I created a section of endnotes to clarify some things for the reader.

Mario Santiago Papasquiaro has two orthographic peculiarities that require mentioning. He avoided the Spanish conjunction "y" ("and") and substituted the ampersand (&). I have followed suit.

In place of "un," "uno" and "una" ("a" and "an"), he uses the numeral one (1). I decided not to do likewise as I was fairly certain that the anglophone reader would assume that, for example, "She was 1 ordinary woman" means "one ordinary woman" instead of "an ordinary woman." I complied with his use of "1" only when it was certain that a numerical singularity was intended.

I want to thank a number of people for their help in this translation project, some for elucidating the meaning of words and phrases, others for explaining who certain people were.

My thanks go to Marta Judit García, Rubén Medina, Richard Belfer, and Juan Felipe Fabre. My heartfelt thanks go to my wife, Christina, for proofreading the manuscript and for her general support and encouragement.

—Arturo Mantecón

Introduction by Ilan Stavans

> A photograph is a secret about a secret, the more it tells you the less you know.
>
> — *Diane Arbus*

In death, he is like an apparition. He shows up inconspicuously, tactfully, in a way he never did in life. No matter how deep you look into his past, you won't find much because most of what he did was impromptu, without a script. He lived in the present, unencumbered, and he left behind a trail of anger and destruction.

He was born in Mexico City in 1953. He called himself Mario Santiago Papasquiaro, although his real name was José Alfredo Zendejas Pineda. He chose his *nom de plume* in part to distinguish himself from the Mexican pop singer José Alfredo Jímenez. His choice, at least some of it, wasn't arbitrary: Santiago Papasquiaro, a town on the slopes of the Sierra Madre in the Mexican state of Durango, was an homage to the purported birthplace of his idol, writer José Revueltas, a political activist and author of the novel *Human Mourning* (1943). Except that Revueltas' siblings were from there, but he was born in a nearby village, Canatlán.

Those who knew Santiago describe his bohemian lifestyle, saying that he was often delirious, wrathful, and abrasive, "*un ser que daba miedo,*" a person at once fearful and frightening. And they recount that he wrote constantly on whatever was at his disposal—napkins, old newspapers, walls. The consensus is that, more than his oeuvre, Santiago himself was a work of art.

From the age of 15, he was an alcoholic. And he died drunk in Mexico City in 1998, after being hit by a car. That's also the year his best friend Roberto Bolaño, whom he hadn't seen for a while, published *The Savage Detectives*, in which Santiago shows up as Ulises Lima, the other savage detective and companion to Arturo Belano, Bolaño's alter ego. The novel is the source of much of Santiago's mythology.

Santiago and Bolaño were the founders and principal promoters of Infrarealism, an aesthetic (also called Visceral Realism) that was also a form of terrorism. Influenced by the Beatnik-inspired counter-culture, it opposed mainstream literature in Mexico City from the 1970s onward, a movement whose members considered Octavio Paz their "great enemy." Some of its members, including Jorge Hernández ("Piel Divina"), Pedro Damián Bautista, Rubén Medina, Mara Larrosa, José Peguero, Bruno Montané, Claudia Kerik, Guadalupe Ochoa, Juan Esteban Harrington, and Mario Raúl Guzmán—all names that with some variations are recognizable to readers of *The Savage Detectives*— would descend on public readings by "Pazitas," the protégés of Paz's circle, disrupting them with horrifying slogans.

Personally, I love *The Savage Detectives* for many reasons, chief among them the fluidity of its style. It is the best Mexican novel of the late 20th century. The fact that it is written by a non-Mexican makes it even more delicious. That Bolaño placed a *lumpen littérateur* at the heart of the period is sheer genius.

Some suggest it is a mistake to let Bolaño set Santiago's agenda. An army of anti-

Bolañistas has coalesced to prove the degree to which— even through the prism of his generosity—Bolaño wasn't altogether kind to Santiago and other Infrarealists. Of course, that Bolaño ended up the chronicler of the movement is the result of sheer ambition. He matured as an artist the way nobody else in his group did: in sustained fashion and in the public eye. But his critics forget that he wrote fiction, not histories.

At any rate, it is essential to return to Santiago, to listen to his voice in unadulterated fashion. Unfortunately, only one slim volume of Santiago's poetry, *Aullido de cisne* (*Swan's Howl*, 1996), as well as a chapbook, *Beso eterno* (*Eternal Kiss*, 1995), were published during his lifetime. And they are virtually impossible to find in print today.

Recognizing his talents, it is known that before Bolaño died in 2003, he was looking for ways to bring out an anthology of his friend's most representative verses. A couple of acquaintances, Juan Villoro and Alejandro Aura, completed the task: the volume, released under the aegis of *Fondo de Cultura Económica* and edited by Santiago's widow, Rebeca López and his Infrarealist friend Mario Raúl Guzmán, is called *Jeta de santo: Antología poética*, 1974-1997 (*Saint's Face*, 2009). It is a valuable compendium. And there is also another one, *Arte & Basura* (*Art & Garbage*, 2013), edited by Luis Felipe Fabre.

It is a measure of Santiago's own estimation that he should remain an apparition. The place where he belongs, the place he fought for, is in the margins. He wasn't a flashy renegade like Bolaño. Any attempt at granting him a more central role betrays his ambition. He was a hell-raiser, *un poeta maldito*, an appellation that comes from Rimbaud, Mallarmé, and Verlaine (*poète maudit*). One never knows what to expect from posterity, but it is my hope that Santiago will remain a footnote, an after-thought, yes, a shadow—like Felisberto Hernández, Calvert Casey, and other *desconocidos*, unknown Latin American authors whose existence comes to us mostly by means of innuendos. Otherwise Santiago's entire enterprise is undermined.

In "Carte d'Identité," an autobiographical poem, Santiago describes himself, in the tradition of Chile's Nicanor Parra, as an "Antipoet & incorruptible idler / fugitive from Nothingness / giant salamander in a cascade of wind."

His third-person self-profile also states that "his profession is: coming to realization, his truth / none at all," and "his fondest dream: putting in a goal from the corner in the flagrant absence of the wind of God, Champion of the Field." Santiago adds: "He writes like he walks / to the rhythm of a barrio brass band / with a steady stride & without let up."

According to his widow and to Mónica Maristain, who wrote a biography of Bolaño, *El hijo de Mister Playa* (*Mister Playa's Son*, 2009), Santiago wrote frantically, maybe even spastically. Poetry was his *raison d'être*. And not just any poetry, but an anxious, automatic poetry without filters, a defiant poetry, a poetry of anger and hallucination that delivers a compulsive anti-establishmentarian stance. He lived dangerously, at all times pushing his mind into the abyss, which is where he believed true art is found.

The literary establishment of the 1970s in Mexico City was stultifying. Even when I came of age a decade later, it was impossible to ignore it. The student massacre in 1968, just as the Olympic Games were about commence, was evidence of a tyrannical ruling party, the PRI (*Partido Revolucionario Institucional*), with little interest in democratic exchange. The PRI held onto power with an iron fist.

Not that dissent was outlawed. You could speak your mind, even on radio, TV, and the printed media. But major industries were tightly controlled by the government. And elections were rigged. Everyone knew it. Mario Vargas Llosa, during a visit, called the system "a perfect dictatorship." (And then he had to leave in a rush.)

You just couldn't do anything about it. In the intellectual and artistic spheres, the division was sharp: either you were with the government or you were against it. If the latter, your chances were slim in terms of exposure. A liberal in his youth, Octavio Paz, fashioned by the PRI as the favorite *intelectual público*, had made a pact with the devil. His personality pretty much resembled that of the ruling party: either you were with him—like historian Enrique Krauze, who ended up assuming Paz's mantle after he died—or you were an enemy.

In other words, the extreme strategies of the Infrarealists were also those of the status quo. It was only natural that people left. Santiago adored Mexico, as he describes in the opening of "In the Gateway of the Clouds":

> My homeland is this juice-laden cactus that I snatched from the very mouth of the desert
> :: Lophophora Williamsii ::
> / Universe of buttons flowering the palms of my hands /
> Leap and dance my destiny
> Like a dog celebrating the punctual blessing of his feeding
> The tongue of God kisses me firmly
> & turns & goes & spins
> devouring the honeycomb of the pupils of my eyes.

Between 1976 and 1978, Santiago lived in Paris, Vienna, Barcelona, and Jerusalem before returning to Mexico City. Bolaño also left—in his case for good—settling in a small town not far from Barcelona (where I met him once). But he couldn't get Santiago out of his mind. Bolaño wrote in his poem entitled, "Burro": "At times I dream that Mario Santiago / Comes to get me, or is a faceless poet, / A head without eyes, or mouth, or nose, / Only skin and will, and I don't ask anything…"

Needless to say, I'm aware of the trap I have set for myself: introducing a volume of Santiago's verses in English translation by Arturo Mantecón defeats the enterprise of secrecy that safeguards Santiago's reputation. The epigraph from Diane Arbus I use at the outset is apt: the best secret is the one not even its owner knows about. I get the impression Santiago was such a combustive artist, his own limits were unknown to him.

My task is not unlike that of the teacher of mysticism, attempting to define or distill the numinous tradition for his students. Mysticism thrives as a secret. It is only for a select group of initiated. Spreading the word about it is an aggression against its very core. Likewise with Santiago's verses: they decidedly aren't for the mainstream. Their themes and cadences are harsh, unpolished, and, well, very visceral, even though I'm the first to recognize it is all a conceit.

For instance, the poems give the appearance of raw spontaneity while they are in fact extraordinary displays of craftsmanship. Look at "3 Seconds Sober & I Go Mad," "I Would Give Everything, Everything, Everything," "Bataille Reincarnate," or "Mallarmé Assaulted," and you see that they work hard at being fresh, unaffected, seemingly unplanned—like the poems of Allen Ginsberg, Neal Cassady, and Kenneth Rexroth. Any other approach would make them pretentious.

Santiago was a poet of chance. He disliked anything remotely resembling a pre-fab structure. Yet there is order to his chaos and structure in his apparent amorphousness. Beauty is freedom, but freedom is the capacity to do as one pleases within certain constraints.

Arguably Santiago's most famous poem—and the war horse in this book—is "Advice from a Disciple of Marx to a Fanatic of Heidegger." A hardboiled existentialism filtered through the prism of Mexican pop culture, peyote trips, and urban alienation, the poem unfolds itself in dialogue with Latin American explorations of the self like those of Ernesto Sábato, Julio Cortázar, and others. Even the epigraph by W.H. Auden (who said, "…poetry makes nothing happen" in his elegy, "In Memory of W.B. Yeats") maps the route the poem is ready to take. Words upside down and inside out: they are everything and nothing. More than a poem, it is a shriek of despair. One is able to recognize the Infrarealist aesthetic, whose message rises like the clenched fist of a manifesto.

Actually, the first line has become a mantra: "The world gives itself to you in fragments / in splinters." The advice of Marx's disciple to Heidegger's fan—that is, from a hyper-materialist to an obfuscating phenomenologist—is rather straightforward: "To live is to hold one's breath."

I'm in awe of Santiago's approach to the Spanish language. You are able to see why Bolaño was such an astounding ventriloquist: he learned the rhythms from his pals. The parlance of Mexico City in the 1970s is superbly invoked here: the innocence, brutality, arbitrariness and poise of sounds forming meaning in an attempt to explain reality, which is nothing but a concoction in the poet's mind while he is simmering in his own mendacity.

Reading Santiago's toils makes me want to scream. The more I read him, the less I know him. He makes me feel as if I'm back in Mexico City, boiling in oil. I regret that I didn't know him. But then again, it is good to get his passion, his luminosity, and his destructiveness tangentially. In a variation of the Diane Arbus view, George Orwell believed that if you want to keep a secret, you must also hide it from yourself. That's the impression one gets from Santiago.

POETRY
COMES
OUT OF MY
MOUTH

Carte d'identité

Si puedes ser leyenda
Para qué ser fosa común

Mario Santiago Papasquiaro / infrarrealista de primera hora ((milita en este movimiento trepidatorio desde su fundación en 1975)) emitió su Aullido de Cisne primigenio en la Ciudad de México —capital de los humillados a raiz— en medio de 1 tormenta eléctrica / la madrugada del 24 de diciembre de 1953 —año de la muerte de Dylan Thomas & Jorge Negrete—.

La cuerda del eco de ese *tour de fórceps a capella* ((bizonte burilado en la placenta de Altamira)) retumba en el violín de Ingres de estas páginas / que a ojo de buen cubero concentran apenas el 10% de los glóbulos rojos de su ópera primate.

Serpiente de agua en el horóscopo chino / *Ocelote* en el náhuatl / *Capricornio* en el occidental / fué en su infancia seguidor de las glorias del *Rebaño Sagrado* del Guadalajara & en su 1a. juventud subía & bajaba ((*sin timón & en el delirio*)) por las serpientes & escaleras escherianas de la *Dialéctica de la Naturaleza* —este desmadre desigual & combinado— con tal impulso / que solo la revelación que le transmitiera el chaneque brigadier José Revueltas: *La tragedia de la especie humana* es *su carencia de sí* lo mantuvo con los pies alados sosteniendo el peso drenado de su cerebelo abierto.

Hoy / mañana & siempre.
Antipoeta & vago insobornable / prófugo de la Nada / ajolote en 1 cascada de aire.
Lo que más ama en la marejada de la vida:
Las hembras platívolas que no cesan de minar la masmédula mítica de los habitantes
de esta galaxia-Oliverio Girondo.
Su profesión es darse cuenta.
Su verdad / ninguna.
Su número teosófico: el 69.
Su *alter ego* / sueño & guía:
Edmundo Dantés / Conde de Montecristo.
Su máxima ilusión: meterle 1 gol de corner a la ausencia flagrante del viento de Dios
Campeador.
Escribe como camina / a ritmo de chile frito.
A tranco firme & sin doblarse.
Entre 1976 & 1978 vivió como chupamirto / olisqueando los puntos cardinales de su
laboratorio aprendizaje: París / Viena / Barcelona & Jerusalem.
Su mujer le dice de cariño: *Ojos de nutria / Boca de glande.*

Carte d'Identité[1]

> If you can be a legend
> Why be a common grave

Mario Santiago Papasquiaro / infrarealist from the very start[2] ((an active member of this ground shaking movement since its founding in 1975)) he let out his primal Swan's Howl in Mexico City —capital of those humiliated to their very roots— in the middle of an electrical storm / the dawn of the 24th of December of 1953 —the year of the death of Dylan Thomas & Jorge Negrete—.[3]

The bowstring of the echo of that *a capella tour de forceps* ((engraved bison in the placenta of Altamira)) resounded on the Ingres violin of these pages / which by educated guess contain barely 10% of the red corpuscles of his primate opera.

Watersnake in the Chinese horoscope / *Ocelot* in the Nahuatl / *Capricorn* in the occidental / in his infancy he was a follower of the glories of the *Sacred Flock* of Guadalajara[4] & in his early youth he went up & went down ((*without rudder & in delirium*)) the Escherian snakes & ladders of the *Dialectics of Nature*[5] —that chaotic disgrace, uneven & mixed— with such an impulsive drive / that only the revelation transmitted to him by the brigadier goblin[6] José Revueltas[7]: *The Tragedy of the Human Species* is *its lack of yes* maintained his winged feet sustaining the drained weight of his open cerebellum.

Today / tomorrow & forever.
Antipoet & incorruptible idler / fugitive from Nothingness / giant salamander[8] in a cascade of wind.
What he loves most in life's heavy seas:
The flying saucer females who do not cease to mine the mythic ultra-marrow of the inhabitants of this Oliverio Girondo[9] galaxy.
His profession is coming to realization.
His truth / none at all.
His theosophical number: 69.
His *alter ego* / dream & guide:
Edmond Dantes / Count of Montecristo.
His fondest dream: putting in a goal from the corner in the flagrant absence of the wind of God, Champion of the Field.
He writes like he walks / to the rhythm of a barrio brass band[10]
With a steady stride & without let up.
Between 1976 & 1978 he lived like a hummingbird / sniffing out the cardinal points of his apprentice's laboratory: Paris / Vienna / Barcelona & Jerusalem.
His wife affectionately calls him: *Otter eyes / Cock tip.*

La poesía sale de mi boca

Para Roberto Bolaño, al que presiento ya como mi Maharischi e iniciador de 1 movimiento cuyo nombre ignoro & en el cual prometo realizarme plenamente

La poesía sale de mi boca,
asoma las narices / el pene
a lo imprevisto /
el estremecimiento
el resplandor /
& la baba también
& los pelos arrancados a este tiempo
a fuerza de jinetearlo
& desatascarle su rodeo /
& la caspa / & la petrificación
de tantas de las yerbas & raíces
de este mundo / que antes de
morderlas nos vemos obligados
a escupir...
La poesía sale de mi boca,
de mis puños, de cada poro
resuelto de mi piel /
de éste mi lugar volátil, aleatorio /
testiculariamente ubicado /
afilando su daga / sus irritaciones
su propensión manifiesta a
estallar / & encender la mecha
en 1 clima refrigerador
donde ni FUS ni FAS
ni mechas ni mechones
   ni 1 sólo constipado
que merezca llamarse constipado,
ni 1 sólo caso de Fiebre-Fiebre
digno de consignarse en este
mi inmóvil país
      La poesía sale de mi boca,
con 1 pelambre & unas antenas
& unos ojos de mosca /
Con los gorjeos de 1 canario
enjaulado / & los bostezos
cacofónicos bostezos del cuidador
del zoológico /
      Noche & día / Roja & negra

Poetry Comes Out of my Mouth

*For Roberto Bolaño,[11] who I feel will become my Maharishi and is the founder of a movement[12]
whose name I am unaware of & in which I pledge to fully realize myself*

Poetry comes out of my mouth,
it juts out from my nostrils / my penis
unexpectedly /
the shuddering
the resplendence /
& drool as well
& my hair now yanked out
by the sheer force of riding it
& pulling out of its deviations /
& dandruff / & the petrification
of so many of the herbs & roots
of this world / that before
taking a bite of them we are obliged
to spit…
Poetry comes out of my mouth,
from my clenched hands, from each resolute
pore of my skin /
from this my volatile, random place /
testicularly located /
sharpening its dagger / its irritations
its manifest propensity to
explode / & light the fuse
in a refrigerator climate
in which it is neither GOOD nor BAD
nor shaggy hanks nor keepsake locks of hair
    nor even a head cold
that merits being called a cold
nor even one single case of Fever-Fever
worthy of being recorded as such in this
my motionless country
   Poetry comes out of my mouth,
with an animal pelt & some antennae
& a few eyes of a fly /
With the warbles of a caged
canary / & the yawns
cacophonous yawns of the
zoo keeper /
    Night & day / Red & black

con los ovarios de 1 muchacha
con la voz ronca de 1 muchacho
con la mirada vacilante
pero rabiosa / hermosamente rabiosa
de 1 niño marica que no
quiere que lo escondan en 1
barril sin fondo
   La poesía sale de mi boca
con la limpia negrura de la gasolina
con el brillo elocuente de 1 foco de 500 voltios
con la emoción & el orgullo
de unos bíceps
   dueños de su mundo
(& dentro de la relatividad
del maestro Einstein):
   Todopoderosos
Con los colores de 1 vestido
hecho con retazos de telas /
con los sonidos confundidos
caóticamente armonizados
de cientos & cientos de cláxons
distintos /
1 día de embotellamiento
en el periférico
   Contra vendavales e inundaciones
(& en cierta manera a
favor de ellos)
 contra casas de puertas cerradas
 contra soles agusanados
 contra cirrosis más allá
 del hígado /
 contra botellas de refresco
 conteniendo urea /
 contra niños & niñas
 castrados / congelados
 el día de su nacimiento /
 contra las toneladas de
 tierra & de basura
 que nos caen encima,
 cuando lo que 1 quiere
 es mostrarse alegre & hermoso
como demostración palpable

with the ovaries of a girl
with the hoarse voice a boy
with the hesitant gaze
but rabid / beautifully rabid
of a queer kid who doesn't
want to be hidden in a
bottomless barrel
       Poetry comes out of my mouth
with the clean blackness of gasoline
with the eloquent brilliance of a 500-volt spotlight
with the excitement & the pride
of some biceps
    masters of their world
(& within the relativity
of master Einstein):
    The all-powerful ones
With the colors of a suit of clothes
made with fabric remnants /
with the confused sounds
chaotically harmonized
of hundreds & hundreds of disparate
car horns /
a day of bottleneck
on the beltway
    Against gale winds & inundations
(& in a certain way a
favor to them)
 against houses with closed doors
 against worm-ridden suns
 against cirrhosis far beyond
the liver /
against soft drink bottles
containing urea /
against boys & girls
castrated / frozen
on the day of their birth /
against the tons of
dirt & garbage
that fall on top of us,
when what one wants
is to show oneself to be happy & beautiful
as a palpable demonstration

de 1 nuevo "renacimiento"
    Saltando & corriendo con los
ágiles/ poniendo 1 cerillo en
el fundillo de los lerdos/
planeando almuerzos & veladas
con los lúcidos /
    poniéndole unas ganas
inmensas a la resolución
de las averías / de Aries a Piscis
de lunes a domingo /
de enero a diciembre
del día 1 al día 31
de tabla apolillada en el piso
a telaraña bailoteando sobre
el techo /
        de reventazón en reventazón
de la impresión de 1 cavernícola
al conocer por 1ª vez a 1
mujer desnuda /
    al último *Ah* de un "fulano
cualquiera", cuando estalle la
3ª Guerra Mundial /
    visitando enfermos
    saludando sanos
conspirando bajotierra
saboteando sobretierra
deteniéndose / avanzando
apurando su trago
saboreándolo
gargareándolo
masajeándoselo
inyectándoselo
        / rascando, rasguñando
        por 1 sol de medianoche
como 2 enamorados excarvándose
como 2 enamorados ensanchando
hasta sus últimas posibilidades
los significantes & el significado
del sistema Braille
como 1 borrachera de
girasoles en círculos / como 1
diadema de dalias la flor

of a new "rebirth"
    Jumping & running with the
agile ones / putting a wax taper in
the asshole of the dimwits /
planning luncheons & soirées
with the bright ones /
    getting immensely
enthused over the resolution
of the malfunctions / from Aries to Pisces
from Monday to Sunday /
from January to December
from the 1st to the 31st
from the worn-out board on the floor
to the spider web shimmying on
the roof /
      of flatulence in flatulence
of the impression of a reactionary
upon meeting for the 1st time
a naked woman /
    the last *Ah* of "somebody
or other," when the 3rd World War
breaks out /
    visiting the sick
    greeting the healthy
conspiring underground
sabotaging above ground
holding back / advancing
hurrying your gulp
savoring it
gargling it
massaging yourself with it
injecting yourself with it
    / scratching, clawing
    by the light of a midnight sun
like 2 lovers digging into each other
like 2 lovers expanding
out to their ultimate possibilities
the signifiers & the signified
of the Braille system
like a drunken binge of
sunflowers in circles / like a
diadem of dahlias the favorite

favorita de Judith /
como 1 toque de mariguana
& tocas el Nirvana con las manos
mueves 1 dedo, & te das cuenta
arrancas el pasto & te sonríes /
gusano de maceta / gusano de
tierra roja que no te conocías /
Como 1 psilocibinazo galopante
que hace harina la piedra
de tus 4 paredes /
& te pone en la proa del cometa Kohoutek
& deja tu jarana al descubierto,
toda tu extensión
tu abreviatura,
     lista a sacudirse /
a no olvidar la cólera justa
por las cabronadas injustas /
sino a enriquecerla
sino a fortificarle
la mecha al TNT,
sino a explotarle
a revirarle la pupila
       Ahora canta el que lloró
hace rato
Grita / Salta / Monta / Eyacula /
el fulano aquel, ya dábanlo
por muerto /
Ahora los cantares duros
las cantatas suaves / las trompetillas
& el regusto de aquel que ha escupido
la tierra & las lagañas
con que habían tapádole los ojos /
     La poesía sale de mi boca
a todo tranco de gerundio
a todo flujo de agua potable
a todo virus luminoso
a toda capacidad de contagio
Así va la poesía /
& para ella
      no tengo sino alabanzas

flower of Judith /
like a hit of marijuana
& you touch Nirvana with your hands
you move a finger, & you realize
you pull up grass & you smile /
flower pot worm / worm of red
earth that you did not know yourself /
Like a huge out of control psilocybin trip
that makes flour out of the rock
of your 4 walls /
& puts you on the prow of the comet Kohoutek
& leaves your sprees & revelry exposed,
your entire expanse
your abbreviation,
        ready to be shaken off /
so as to not forsake the proper cholera
for the unjust dirty tricks /
but rather to enrich
but rather to strengthen
the fuse to the TNT,
to explode it
to make the pupil of your eye turn inward
        Now he sings who wept
a short time ago
Shouts / Leaps / Mounts / Ejaculates /
that So & So whom they had given up
for dead /
Now the hard ballads
soft cantatas / Bronx cheers
& the aftertaste for him who has spit out
the earth & the mucous
with which his eyes had been sealed /
        Poetry comes out of my mouth
in full gerundial coin
in full flow of potable water
in full viral luminosity
in full capacity of contagion
So it goes with poetry /
& for her
        I have nothing but praises

Para nuestra Señora de Guadalumpen

Por el manto cumbiambero de mi virgen
por su sexy morenía
por su aparición tan espectral
en el tiempo en el que herraban
los corazones de mi savia
& los cerros se cubrían de gemidos e impiedad

Por el halo de tzentzontles con que hablaba
Cantadito como en barrio lagunero
o en fandango de nopal
Negra perla / faz briosa
Mancha húmeda
he venido estas "Mañanitas" a clamar
Mexicanos de hasta abajo
teoyótls desvanecidos
desde el cráter de la herida
la venimos a invocar

No que perros la transporten
o en la feria de su espíritu se revenda el nanacátl
Nuestra entrega es flor sedosa
Guerra abierta a la boñiga del corral

Por mirar de frente su solar descompostura
larva ella que trastorna
la severa senilidad de los magueyes
agua regia que bebemos
como a vulva de panal
Niña ella de los cielos
travesura-sed embriagapuertas
A los pies de su misterio
nos venimos a inclinar
Quiera la raíz de nuestro ojo no negarla ni evadirla
Arde su ala / la llamarada de su brisa
Su petate es mi petate
Nuestra boda / celestial

For Our Lady of Guadalumpen[13]

By the cumbia-girl cape of my virgin
by her sexy brown skin
by her so spectral apparition
in the time in which they branded
the hearts of my life blood sap
& the hills were blanketed with groans and impiety

By the halo of mockingbirds with which she spoke
In sing-song accents heard in lowly barrio
or in a cactus fandango
Black Pearl / animated face
Damp stain
I have come to clamor these "Mañanitas"[14]
Mexicans of the lowest station
divine spirits vanished
from the crater of the wound
we come to invoke her

May dogs not carry her
nor magic mushrooms be sold in the festive market of her spirit
Our offering is a silken flower
Open war on the cow shit of the corral

By looking straight at her solar discomposure
she becomes a larva that drives mad
the severe senility of the agaves
aqua regia that we drink
like honeycomb pussy
She, girl-child of the heavens
is mischief-thirst of drunken doors
At the feet of her mystery
we come to bow
She wants the root of our eye to not deny her nor evade her
Burning is her wing / the sudden flame of her tender wind
Her woven palm mat is my mat of palm[15]
Our wedding / celestial

Confesión de Juan Diego

Hay tiempo para el llanto
& tiempo para patear el llanto

Ramón Martínez Ocaranza

Siento la cabeza / como la piedra de la honda con que David tiró a Goliat
Me llamo Juan Diego
　　　　—Mariposa Izcuintli—
& el rocío de la Subida
se me confunde con la locura viva de los pájaros
Trepo el cerrito de mi día tras otro
Aunque hoy huele a huerta en el zaguán
El frío es de alas de segundos desplegados
Converso con mi último pulquito
/ Gajo de raíz de noche blanca /
& mi abuela pulpa de frijol
Es de madrugada
El Cielo & la Tierra se maridan
: Abriéndose a raíz :
Escucho 1 voz / Cual si naciera
Las laderas de mi Paso
al Este & al Oeste se unen
sosteniéndole el rostro a mi visión
Es de mujer la luz que hoy me alcanza
Su olor a tamarindo me atrapa sin herir
Me dice / lo que yo ya me decía
　　　　　en bruscos sueños /
Pero esto: ¡Por la Tierra de Fuego que hoy piso!:
es respirar en agua clara el viento hermano de mi Dios
& levitando & tropezando me reintegro
Beso el cáliz de esta imagen tan cercana
Musito Tonantzin / sin abrir la boca
No seré el mismo
Pero nunca *El Otro*
Los días que transcurran incubarán por siempre este momento
& los hijos de mis hijos transmitirán a su manera mi visión

Confession of Juan Diego[16]

> There is a time for weeping
> & a time to give weeping the boot
>
> *Ramón Martínez Ocaranza*

My head feels / like the rock from the sling that David flung at Goliath
My name is Juan Diego
                    —Butterfly Dog—[17]
& I mistook the dew of the Ascent
for the living madness of the birds
I scale the little hill of my day after day
Even though today there is a smell of orchard in the portal
The cold consists of wings of unfolded moments
I converse with my last quick drink of pulque
/ Root segment of a pale sleepless night /
& my grandmother, flesh of frijol
It is early in the morning
The Sky & the Earth are wedded
: Opening up from the root :
I hear a voice / As though I were just born
The flanking slopes of my Pass
to the East & to the West become one
keeping the face in my sight
The light that now reaches me belongs to a woman
Her scent of tamarind ensnares me harmlessly
She says to me / what I have already said to myself
                        in brief rude dreams /
But this: by the Land of Fire I walk on!:
is breathing in clear water the wind-brother of my God
& levitating & stumbling I make myself whole again
I kiss the calyx of this oh so near image
I mutter Tonantzin[18] / without opening my mouth
I will not be the same
But will never be *The Other*
The days to come will nurture this moment forever
& my children's children will transmit my vision in their own way

Canción implacable

Me cago en Dios
& en todos sus muertos
Me cago en la hostia
& en el coñito de la virgen
Me cago en los muertos
del Dios de Dios
en la soberbia de Federico Nietzsche
en el cuerpo tembloroso de mi alma
& en las ortigas al aire del ateo
en la muerte prematura de los justos
en la fugacidad del coito & sus centellas
En el verbo animal
En la imaginación-rizoma
En los textos del saber tan destetado
En la raja de los mundos
Yo me cago
Concentrado en el incendio de mis poros
en este alcohol-maleza que me cimbra
en el ojo infinito de mis huellas
en el furor salvaje del desmadre
en la imposible muerte & sus ofrendas
En el barro del áspid que calienta
en las rocas de la amada
en la levitación de mi calaca
en el cojo corazón de lo innombrable
En el aleph acuoso de mis llagas
en la vítrea desazón de mi asesino
en la mano del placer
en la droga anidada en sus colmillos
En el ogro filantrópico & su esposa
en la tumba del azar tan manoseada
en el germen de la lírica / que es caca
En la boñiga aérea
en las lagañas topas
en el cráneo todo resplandor de Charleville
En las ratas que aún huyen del Mar Ebrio
en lo blando
en lo fofo
& en lo inerme

Implacable Song

I shit on God
& on all of his dead
I shit on the communion host
& the virgin's little cunt
I shit on the dead
of the God of God
on the master morality of Friedrich Nietzsche
on the trembling body on my soul
& on the exposed nettles of the atheist
on the premature death of the righteous
on the fleeting nature of coitus & its flash
On the animal verb
On rhizome-like imagination
On the texts of fully weaned wisdom
On the ass crack of the planets
I shit
Concentrating on the wildfire of my pores
on this alcohol undergrowth that thrashes me
on the infinite eye of my footprints
on the savage fury of shameful chaos
on impossible death & its offerings
On the mud of the asp that suns itself
on the rocks of the beloved
on the levitation of my skull & bones
on the lame heart of the unspeakable
On the aqueous aleph of my stigmata
on the vitreous rash of my assassin
on the hand of pleasure
on the drug wedged in his front teeth
On the philanthropic ogre & his wife
on the wretched grave of chance
on the germ of lyrical poetry / which is a turd
On the airborne horseshit
on the sleep sand in the eyes of moles
on the all-splendored cranium of Charleville
On the rats still fleeing from the Drunken Sea
on the soft
on the flabby
& on the defenseless

En el eructo del éter de los sapos
en las sangres hirvientes
en las sombras
en el rosa gargajo de las albas
en el vidrio insensato que he escogido como calle
en las barrancas de Venus tumefacta
En el platón del festín
en las bacinicas de la tregua
en el hongo podrido & su tridente
En el genealógico tumor de la US Army
en el extenso linaje de la mierda
Abismo & resplandor / azar & viento
Vena abierta de cocxis a clavícula
Regazo de embriaguez
/ Llama de arpas embozadas
En las ingles sin axilas de Dios-inventamuertos
en el suave & múltiple rumor que hacen 2 lágrimas
 : en el mar : en sus desiertos :
& en mí mismo

On the toads' belch of ether
on boiling blood
on the shadows
on the pink phlegm of the daybreak
on the insensate glass I have chosen for a road
in the canyons of swollen Venus
On the banquet platter
in the little chamber pots of the ceasefire
on the rotten toadstool & its trident
On the genealogical tumor of the US Army
on the extensive lineage of shit
Abyss & resplendency / chance & wind
Open vein from coccyx to clavicle
Lateness of pregnancy
/ Flame of muffled harps
On groins without the armpits of God-inventorofthedead
on the suave & multiple murmur made by 2 teardrops
 : on the sea : on its deserts :
& on myself

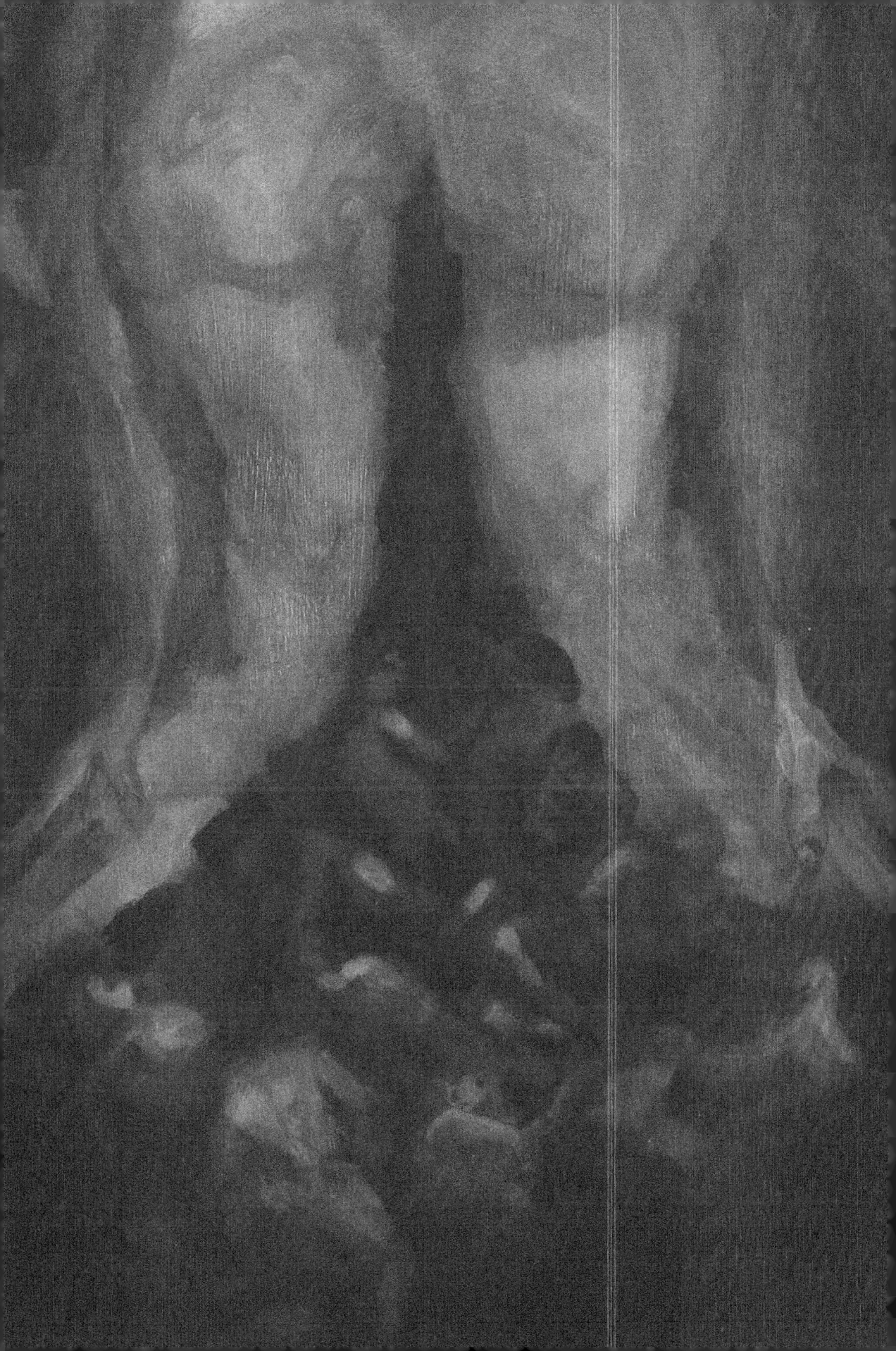

3 segundos sobrio y enloquezco

¡Secas / las piedras!

Húmedo —como las panochas & las vergas tragadas de ansiedad—

Hundió mi hocico en la boca de la fuente de la embriaguez que no se raja

Ni me bamboleo ni taloneo para la otra

La madre & las hermanas de Baco chupan de mi propia sangre

/ & a mi ritmo /

La agonía & el éxtasis se apuntan

Infierno & Paraíso se dejan de jaladas

& se tiran a vivirme / ¡hasta el final!

Si hoy es mezcal o mera lluvia

Si flujo de mujer o lágrimas babeadas en la espina de la desesperación

Ese choque a contraluz de los opuestos penetra en la pechuga / en el guano

En el sagrado licor de mi comprensión e incomprensión

Cabalgo / nado / prendido de la reata de Ariadna del alcohol

Él es mi caleidoscopio : mi AK 47 : mi ausencia & mi presencia

El garañón en el que montan miradas de perras rojas

En lo alto de la noche que cintila

3 Seconds Sober and I Go Mad

Dry / the stones!
Damp —like the pussies & the cocks engulfed by anxiety—
My snout sank into the source of the fount of unrepentant drunkenness
I neither wavered nor punked out for the other
The mother & sisters of Bacchus sucked my own blood
/ & to my own rhythm and beat /
Agony & ecstasy are at the ready
Inferno & Paradise quit their bullshitting
& strive to keep me alive / until the end!
If today it's mezcal or mere rain
Whether the flow of a woman or tears wept and dribbled on the thorn of desperation
That back-lit clash of opposites pierces the breast / the bird shit
In the sacred liquor of my comprehension and incomprehension
I gallop / I swim / seized by the Ariadne lasso of alcohol
It is my kaleidoscope : my AK 47 : my absence & my presence
The stallion ridden by the stares and gazes of red dogs
In the utmost of the glimmering night

En el zaguán de las nubes

Para Patricia Rodríguez Acosta

> Porque todos somos,
> todos somos,
> todos somos los hijos de,
> todos somos los hijos de
> 1 brillante & colorida flor,
> 1 flor llameante
> & no hay nadie
> no hay nadie
> que lamente lo que somos
>
> *Canción huichola*

Mi patria es este cacto jugoso que arranco de la boca misma del desierto
  :: *Lophophora Williamsii* ::
/ Universo de botones floreando las palmas de mis manos /
Salta & danza mi destino
como 1 perro celebrando la bendición puntual de su alimento
La lengua de Dios me besa con firmeza
& torna & sigue & gira
devorando el panal de mis pupilas
Está lloviendo
& la huella del diluvio
no es otra que la tierra que hoy piso
A la distancia
sólo veo el pálpito fruto vivo de mi alma
Mis abuelos —peregrinos— me indican el camino / pellizcándome
El sudor de mis moléculas
prende el sueño necesario
para que la intrínseca ceguera de mis pies
no decaiga ni en brújula ni en ánimo
La realidad de la belleza
  ((luciérnaga fugaz))
se posa 1 segundo en mis cabellos
¿Qué viento negro podría romperme el paso
o intentar siquiera cancelar mi canto?
El vientre de mis dientes no deja de masticar su propia pulpa
Vuelo : trino : zureo : aúllo : salpico: preño : me exprimo : me desato
Llevo en mí el eco de 1 impulso insospechable
Simiente lunar / manantial de migraciones

In the Gateway of the Clouds

For Patricia Rodríguez Acosta

> Because we are all,
> we are all,
> we are all the children of,
> we are all the children of
> a brilliant and colorful flower,
> a blazing flower
> & there is no one
> there is no one
> who laments what we are
>
> *Huichol[19] song*

My homeland is this juice-laden cactus I snatched from the very mouth of the desert
  :: *Lophophora Williamsii* ::[20]
/ Universe of buttons flowering the palms of my hand /
Leap and dance my destiny
like a dog celebrating the punctual blessing of his feeding
The tongue of God kisses me firmly
& turns & goes & spins
devouring the honeycomb of the pupils of my eyes
It is raining
& the imprint of the flood
is none other than the land on which I tread
In the distance
I see only the living fruit pulse of my soul
My grandparents —pilgrim migrants— point out the road to me / pinching me
The sweat of my molecules
ignites the necessary dream
to the intrinsic blindness of my feet
so as not to languish in compass or in spirit
The reality of beauty
     ((fugitive firefly))
alights for 1 second in my hair
What black wind would rend my path
or at least attempt to cancel my song?
The belly of my teeth does not stop chewing its own flesh
I fly : I warble : I coo : I howl : I spatter : I impregnate : I milk myself : I let myself go
I carry within me the echo of an unforeseeable impulse
Lunar seed / fountainhead of migrations

arcilla lodazal de óvulos / visiones & peñascos
raíz que surge & se evapora
En el zaguán de las nubes
A la luz del relámpago
A 1 salto de besar el alba-pezuña de venado
que acaricia el dulce corazón de Wirikuta

muddy clay of ovules / visions & rocky crags
root that emerges & evaporates
In the gateway of the clouds[21]
In the light of a thunderbolt
In a leap to kiss the dawning-hoof of the stag
that caresses the sweet heart of Wirikuta[22]

Nosotros / que por doquiera buscamos la aventura

Para Álvaro Carrillo

De Avignon / ya sé que sólo voy a recordar
aquellas horas en que sus murallas-camisón de fuerza
se venían abajo con tus besos / & la luz
contenida-enjaulada entre la hierba de esos campos
que volvieron loco, pintor, sordo inimitable, nervioso mulo rojo
a ese tranquilo campesino que algún día fue Van Gogh
Pero qué importa la arbitraria taquigrafía de la historia de haches mudas
en estos puentes, donde la iluminación súbita, el hastío, la pasión,
fueron las ratas / la avalancha ácida-espumosa que decidieron en verdad
nuestros repentinos electrocutantes despegues de este suelo
donde los normales hubieran querido que sólo transitaran
los autos de patas zambas / los escarabajos más tarados
Exactamente sobre estas mismas carreteras
donde vagábamos, nos asoleábamos, nos despeñábamos tú & yo
buscando vino, ¡francos!, oportunidades de sudar en la vendimia;
mientras en alguna otra coladera, recámara, bar de 4 tragos
  1 querido compita paranoico se volvía loco —nudo de lágrimas saladas—
                        dándonos por muertos
& corría, aullaba, preguntaba / de 1 muelle a 1 cueva, de la comisaría al hospital,
    describiendo hasta las patas de las moscas que por las tardes solían tomar cerveza
    en nuestros ojos

Pero todavía no era la hora de truequear nuestra energía
  por 1 campito desyerbado entre las paralíticas piernas de la Nada
Amor / Amor / Amor / & no sólo complejo de papalotes chinos
  eran el motor & la carnada que nos hacía saltar
del silencio, la oscuridad o el dulce sleepingbag
  como chapulines con resorte

El aire ágil como 1 puma o 1 mesero acostumbrado
  a servir con elegancia el cristal, la dinamita de las grandes
     borracheras
la neblina de 6 alas & l0 lenguas
  o las conversaciones que a veces eran verdaderos aguaceros, rajaduras de la Tierra,
servían de almohada, de linterna, de afrodisíaco, de mantel
              / Sacudían / hechizaban /

We / Who Look for Adventure Anywhere

For Álvaro Carrillo[23]

Of Avignon / I already know that I will only recall
those hours in which its straitjacket walls
fell to the ground with your kisses / & the light
encaged-contained amid the vegetation of those fields
that drove mad that painter, inimitably deaf, that nervous red mule
that tranquil peasant who one day would become Van Gogh
But of what importance is the arbitrary stenography of the history of mute H's
on those bridges, where sudden illumination, weariness, passion,
were the rats / the foaming acid avalanche that truly decided
our precipitous electrocuting lift-offs from this earth
where the normal ones have only wanted to travel by
bow-legged autos / the most defective beetles
Precisely on these same highways
upon which we bummed around, sunned ourselves, tripped & fell you & I
searching for wine (francs!), opportunities to sweat in the grape harvest;
while in some other culvert, bedroom, four-drink bar
  a dear paranoid pal goes crazy —a knotted lump of salty tears—
                                giving us up for dead
& he ran around, howled, questioned / a cave about a wharf, asked for the police
    station at the hospital
describing even the feet of the flies that in the evening would drink up the beer in our
    eyes

But it was still not the time to barter our energy
  for a weed-plucked field between the paralytic legs of Nothingness
Love / Love / Love / & not just a complex of Chinese kites
  was the motor & the lure that made us leap
out of silence, the darkness or the sweet sleeping bag
  like grasshoppers on springs

The air as nimble as a puma or a waiter accustomed
  to serving the crystal with elegance, the dynamite of great
    drunken binges
the fog of 6 wings & 10 tongues
  or the conversations that at times were true cloudbursts, ruptures in the Earth,
serving as pillow, as lantern, as aphrodisiac, as table cloth
              / They shocked / they bewitched /

& nosotros no necesitábamos sino dejar que nuestra sangre
esculpiera sus propios faros, sus propios rompeolas
su alfabeto hecho de nuestras manos exploradoras
        & nuestras respiraciones ruidosísimas

el mundo podía acabar en el próximo autostop
  en la fantasmal inspección de documentos migratorios
    en la búsqueda del siguiente árbol de haschisch
con cualquier muslo o cabellera color miel
  que quisieran romper cagarrutear
    la absurda escultura monogámica / que habíamos tejido
      con la menstruación & las ganas de jugar de nuestros cuerpos

La hora propicia para el amor & sus túneles del tiempo (te apuesto todo mi vino de
    este mes)
no nos las dio Avignon ni su larga cabellera de albas & uvas rosadas
ni el lento zumbante vacío que arrugaba tus jeans & a mí me apaleaba los ojos
  me levantaba la piel & me ponía a cantar catatónicos
    corridosmexicanos
    con 1 voz aguardientosamente parecida a pegamento de zapatos
      a cagada de caballo de San Luis, a relámpago destripador de cielos
        a cactus rocoso (nada almibarado) perro provocador de
          imágenes & gags
          nitidaepilépticamente más allá del cine mudo
        en 1 especie de altamar existencial al que 1 cariñosamente
          siempre apodará como el regreso del Potiemkin

Lejos aún & hasta eso cerca de la hora del vómito el calambre & el desgarre
  de la seca mañana en la que tuve que separarme de tu cuerpo
    pero sin decirte *Adeu* / ni *Aquí se chingó el esplendor*

& we needed nothing more than to let our blood
carve out its own lighthouses, its own breakwater
its alphabet made by our exploring hands
        & our most loud noisy breathing

the world might have ended in the next hitchhike
  in the phantasmal inspection of migratory documents
    in the search for the next tree of hashish
with whatever honey-colored thigh or hair
  that would want to break up shitting out
    the absurd monogamous sculpture / that we had put together
      with the menstruation & the craving of our bodies for play

The propitious hour for love & its time tunnels (I wager you all my wine for this
      month)
Avignon gave us neither its long tresses of dawns & rosy grapes
nor the slow humming void that wrinkled your jeans & thrashed my eyes
  it lifted my skin off & set me to singing catatonic
      Mexican corridos
    with a firewater voice similar to adhesive for shoes
      to a dump from a St. Louis horse, to a lightning bolt gutting the heavens
        to a rock cactus (not at all gentle) dog provocateur of
          images & gags
          crystalclearepileptically well beyond the silent cinema
          in a species of existential high sea that one affectionately
            will always call the return of the Potiemkin

Still far away & even at that close to the time of vomit electric shock & spasm
  of the stark morning in which I had to take leave of your body
    but without telling you *Adieu* / or *Here it was that splendor was fucked*

Daría todo todo todo

(A la manera de Richard Belfer / joven poeta francés)
Para Mara Larrosa
Michel et Adeline Bulteau

Daría todo por morir prendido de los labios de Marlene
La niña sueño & maravilla
                         que pedía autostop
frente al museo Gustav Moreau en las afueras de París
la que era un caramelo una tarabilla
                         1 tranvía caudaloso / Platicando /
& se reía de la manera como miraba sus medias negras
con entusiasmo con verdadero entusiasmo
& Michel hablaba de astrología & vibraciones
que llevamos en nuestro protoplasma nuestro propio Maharishi
& Marlene estaba allí
presente como el agua ruidosa
que rodaba del Norte al Sur del parabrisas
& comenzaban a meter las narices
la telepatía & esa especie de imán
que nosotros por no parecer pedantes llamamos simpatía
& de repente no sé por qué
comenzamos a jugar a las cosquillas
El roedor del lado Sur de nuestro cerebro
se sentía gato borracho por el Gozo
& los vientres / qué piruetas no hacían los vientres
más / más / exigían más
como si estuviéramos buceando
por 1ª vez en estas aguas
& para entonces el cuerpo & la mente de Marlene
ya bailaban
en el patio de mi cuerpo & de mi mente
nuestras respiraciones se acariciaban en la misma cama
nuestros 4 labios en pandilla
se decían poemas que sólo el animal desnudo entiende
Marlene Marlene tierna festiva sabia loca fraternal
Así fuiste Marlene
las 5 horas & media que duró el trayecto
las 5 horas & media que fueron una planta
de otra vida sembrada en la huerta de esta vida

I Would Give Everything Everything Everything

(After the manner of Richard Belfer[24] / young French poet)
For Mara Larrosa[25]
Michel and Adeline Bulteau

I would give everything to die fastened to the lips of Marlene
The dream girl & marvel
     who thumbed a ride
in front of the Gustave Moreau museum on the outskirts of Paris
she who was a sweet thing a chatterbox
     a free-flowing streetcar / Chatting /
& she laughed at the way I gazed at her black stockings
with enthusiasm with true enthusiasm
& Michel talked about astrology & vibrations
that we carry in our protoplasm our own Maharishi
& Marlene was there
as present as the noisy water
that rolled from North to South off the windshield
& they started to butt in
telepathy & that sort of magnet
that not wanting to seem pedantic we call sympathy
& suddenly I don't know why
we started to tickle each other
The rodent from the South side of our brain
felt like a drunken cat due to the Delight
& our guts / there was no end to what pirouettes our guts made
more / more / they demanded more
as though we were diving
for the 1st time in these waters
& by then the body & the mind of Marlene
were dancing
in the courtyard of my body & my mind
our breaths caressed in the same bed
our four lips ganged up
speaking poems that only the naked animal would understand
Marlene Marlene tender festive wise mad fraternal
That was how you were Marlene
the 5 & a half hours the trajectory lasted
the 5 & a half hours that were a plant
from another life sown in the garden of this life

& qué pupilas & qué tacto & qué ritmo tendrías
en qué parques habrás jugado / en qué subterráneos
u orillas de lagos habrás menstruado
o comido cerezas silvestres camarada Marlene
que hace 6 meses no deseo otra cosa
que morir como bonzo & prendido a tus labios
vestidos los 2 de milicianos cubanos o de juglares medievales
& cantando a Dylan si quieres & bailando con Hendrix
& haciendo el amor

& what eyes & what touch & what rhythm would you have
in what parks would you have played / in what undergrounds
or lakesides would you have menstruated
or have eaten wild cherries comrade Marlene
so it is now 6 months that I have desired no other thing
than to die like a self-immolating suicide & affixed to your lips
the two of us dressed like Cuban militia or medieval minstrels
& singing to Dylan if you want & dancing to Hendrix
& making love

Correspondencia infra

El mar toca nuestros cuerpos
para sentir su cuerpo
Lo mismo en Manzanillo pedregoso
que en Neviot / isla de corales del desierto
Nosotros devolvemos su sonrisa de sal
dibujando nuestros nombres & apetencias
en el caparazón de los cangrejos
que parecen buscar viejas patas de palo devoradas por la arena
El mar se para de cabeza
& nos canta / en el idioma más desnudo & afín a nuestro tacto
Port Vendrés Ville ruge como atún encolerizado en nuestros ojos
Bernard prende 1 de sus aretes verde flúor en la cabellera
  alfilereada de 1 erizo
Los demás pescadores del *Saint Joan / Fetiche II*
desde sus camarotes se sinceran a su modo
con éste también su mar que los filma fijamente
Ahí donde ellos se aflojan su nervioso pantalón
& sus labios no dejan de ulular
cuando ven hasta las anginas del Peñón de Gibraltar
moviéndose como dados o peces plateados
en la sombra de sus vasos de ron

Infra Correspondence

The sea touches our bodies
in order to feel its own body
The same in rocky Manzanillo
as in Neviot / island of desert corals
We return its smile of salt
tracing our names & cravings
on the carapace of crabs
that seem to search out old wooden legs eaten away by the sands
The sea stands on its head
& sings to us / in the most naked idiom related to our sense of touch
Port-Vendrés Ville bellows in our eyes like a choleric tuna
Bernard fastens 1 of his fluoride-green earrings to the spiny tresses of a sea urchin
The rest of the fisherman of the *Saint Joan / Fétiche II*
display sincerity in their own fashion from their boat cabins
and this with their sea that steadfastly films them
There where they loosen their ill at ease trousers
& their lips do not cease to ululate
when they look out toward the adenoids of the Rock of Gibraltar
moving about like dice or silvery fish
in the shadows of their glasses of rum

Sinaí

Carpa beduina
Bendición de sombras
A la hora en que raja leña el ojo omnisciente del s-o-l
Arca que flotas entre las dunas
Alucinación radiante
Pellejo de dromedario
Opio salvaje
Poro a poro el desierto es tuyo & te sostiene
Ceca & Meca
Remolino silencioso
Cópula pedregosa
Esculpida frente a la demencia del mar
Haschisch de luna creciente
Casamata del amor & la aventura
Rojísima zarza
Piedra de toque zaraza

Sinai

Bedouin tent
Blessing of shadows
At the hour when kindling is cut the omniscient eye of the s-u-n
The ark that you float among the dunes
Radiant hallucination
Dromedary hide
Wild opium
Pore to pore the desert is yours & it sustains you
Pillar to Post
Silent dust devil
Stony copulation
Sculpted before the dementia of the sea
Crescent moon hashish
Fortified house for love & adventure
Bramble most red
Calico touchstone

Visión en El Sinaí

Para Esther Cameo & Mauri Pilatowski

El vagabundo-ojos de iguana / pasó por aquí
& su sudor lo huelen todavía los vientos
los dioses-sangre de camello que habitan e iluminan el corazón de estas montañas
Las tribus de pastores de Beersheva
aún extrañan el canto lleno de ecos de sus botas
el fogonazo de su piel / tan parecida a 1 reata de muelle
con los mismos vaivenes de 1 salivazo de Arak
A la hora de los dátiles
los crepúsculos lentos / los fervorosos sorbos al jocoque
Agua noble le dicen en su dialecto los beduinos
& dibujan: 1 árbol con ropas colgando
                    1 casa con alas en la arena
El vagabundo-ojos de iguana / pasó por aquí
& parecía 1 de esos rayos que escribían sin necesidad de olivettis-letteras & sin lápices
palabras capaces de dar cuerda al músculo azul de los patriarcas & sus pueblos
El vagabundo de lengua extrañísima
el cantador de cucurrucucús & ayayays
—al que seguían como a mancha de petróleo
los paracaidistas los radares israelíes—
El de las mejillas de cactus
el de los cigarros trepadores
el bebedor de escalofríos
el explorador de labios submarinos
el que se llevaba de *Salaam Aleko*
hasta con el seco vozarrón de las palmeras
El de la calaverita sonriente
grabada a punta de arañazos
en el hueso-vida perpetua de su mochila de viaje
Él / que besaba la rarísima llegada de las lluvias
& se abría como sólo la tierra pocas veces
& se abría / como si en ese momento todos nos fuéramos a morir

Vision in Sinai

For Esther Cameo & Mauri Pilatowski[26]

He with the vagabond eyes of an iguana / passed through here
& his sweat is still smelt by the winds
the camel blood gods that inhabit and illuminate the heart of these mountains
Even the shepherd tribes of Bersheva
miss the song filled with the echoes of his boots
the fireflash of his skin / so similar to a mooring line
with the same fluxes of a gob of spat-out Arak
At the hour of the palm dates
the slow twilights / the fervid mouthfuls of sour milk
Called *Noble water* in the dialect of the Bedouins
& in the sand they draw: 1 tree with ropes hanging from it
                    1 house with wings
He with the vagabond eyes of an iguana / passed through here
& he seemed one of those lightning bolts that wrote without need of Olivetti
    Letteras & without pencils
words capable of winding the blue muscle of the patriarchs & their peoples
The vagabond of the strangest tongue
the singer of coo-coo-roo-coo-coos & ayayays
—who was tailed like an oil streak
by the Israeli paratroopers & radars
He of the cactus cheeks
he of the creeper vine cigars
the drinker of cold sweats
the explorer of submarine lips
he who got by with *Salaam Aleko*
even with the dry booming voice of the palm trees
He of the small smiling skull
engraved drypoint with spidery scratches
on the perpetual life-bone of his rucksack
He / who kissed the most seldom arrival of the rains
& opened up as only the earth has ever done
& opened up / as though in that moment all of us were going to die

La última balada del sol

(Para ser cantada en la boca-granada abierta del Metro)

> What sage in the darkness?
>
> *Allen Ginsberg*

I

Qué muchacha
nos acompañará
en estas madrugadas / casi muertas
bajo este viento
½ animal / ½ estatua
(70% guacamaya disecada)
qué muchacha nos acompañará
qué revólver
qué canción

II

¿Será 1 *hoguera tribal*
la cáscara alborotada de sus muslos?
¿1 florero-aroma de gladiolas
la varita de incienso de su clítoris?
¿Aparecerá el pueblofantasma de mi boca
entre las rocas de sus mapas genitales?
¿entre la excitación-caleidoscopio de sus fuegos pálidos?
¿Arderá en ella el altamar?
¿Los cromosomas de sus veleros tendrán alas?

III

Qué muchacha nos asoleará
ahora que la sangre nos es tinta
taquicardia de octopus hechizado
porque la música-hacha de piedra de los *Who*
estampada a las ubres de 1 espectro verde
se acerca sonajeando irremediablemente
1 claro presagio de adrenalina arapantanos

The Last Ballad of the Sun

(To be sung in the open grenade-mouth of the Metro)

What sage in the darkness?
Allen Ginsberg

I

What girl
will accompany us
on these early mornings / almost dead
under this wind
½ animal / ½ statue
(70% stuffed macaw)
what girl will accompany us
what revolver
what song

II

Will the shaken shell of her thighs
be a *tribal bonfire*?
the incense stick of her clitoris
a flower shop aroma of gladiolas?
Will the ghost town of my mouth appear
among the rocks of her genital maps?
amidst the kaleidoscope arousal of her pallid fires?
Will the high seas burn within her?
Will the chromosomes of her sailing ships have wings?

III

What girl will cure us in the sun
now that blood is for us
tachycardial ink of a bewitched octopus
because the stone axe-music of the *Who*
embossed on the udders of a green specter
unavoidably draws near tambourine jangling
a clear foretelling of swamp-plowing adrenaline

IV

What sage in the darkness?
        dice Allen Ginsberg
/ qué pedo : qué explosión
en las salidas de emergencia /
Camino al *Desolations Pub*
Camino a la *Inconciencias Factory*
Cuál entre todas las muchachas
va a ser la que se acerque primero con su pezón derecho
& 1 flor del diablo subrayándole los ojos
¿La encontraremos pelándonos sus órbitas
exigiendo 1 poro más de ácido & naranjas
en plena Piazza De Navonna
en el Cuadrante de la Soledad mexicanito?
¿Saludará con 1 *dejémoslo todo / nuevamente*?
¿Invitará a 1 safari sin escalas al interior de su torta mordisqueada?
Qué salud : qué verdad : qué tenaza de cangrejo
qué verso de Msses Adriane Rich la oiremos inyectarnos
¿Será ella 1 hija inconfundible
de Frank Zappa & Nina Hagen?
¿Bongocearán sus labios
himnos / maldiciones / epilepsias?
¿respiraciones que sólo se dan
cuando baja sus cortinas el pulmón de 1 loco?
Qué muchacha nos acompañará
            lava abajo
hacia el fin del fin
del callejón

IV

What sage in the darkness?
   says Allen Ginsberg
/ what stink of a fight : what explosion
in the emergency exits /
On the way to *Desolation Pub*
On the way to the *Oblivions Factory*
Which among all the girls
will be the one who will come near with her right nipple
& a devil flower underlining her eyes
Will we find her skinning her eye sockets for us
demanding one more pore of acid & oranges
in the middle of the Piazza De Navonna
in the little Mexican Quadrant of Solitude?
Will she greet us with a *let's leave it all alone / yet again*?
Will she invite us on a non-stop safari to the interior of her nibbled sandwich?
What health : what truth : what crab pincer
With what verse of Ms. Adrienne Rich will we hear her inject us
Will she be an unmistakable daughter
of Frank Zappa & Nina Hagen?
Will her lips bongo us
hymns / maledictions / epilepsies?
breaths that are let out only
when the lung of a madman lowers her curtains?
What girl will accompany us
       lava underneath
toward the end of the end
of the alley

San Juan de la Cruz le da 1 aventón a Neal Cassidy / en la frontera entre el mito & el sueño

La carretera se pandea rumbo al centro de su propio
                         incendio centrífugo
Tijuana se desvanece flotando bajo la mollera del ojo
Esquirlas de cabaret & colchón empujan la estela
de duendes que preña la ilusión de este instante
En el radio: Jim Morrison traga esporas crecidas
                   en la cicatriz del diluvio
Este puente mental va al volante
Estrellado el afuera & adentro
Verde mota la selva
El destino rodando
Todo ser & hasta en zancos escupe ovnis bordados
con alas de las más locas luciérnagas
Es de noche / & en carretera / & volando
Los Doors con los dientes hacen realidad su voltaje
El cuerpo del alma se baña en el viaje
El centro se curva
La curva es salvaje
La carretera es Dios mismo
Cada ganglio / cada trozo
resbala: se esfuma
El pie va braceando
La mente desyerba la euforia del eco
El asesino sonámbulo cruzó los portales de la pesadilla vacía
Nevaba en la azorada noche de abril
La huelga de basura había llegado a sus sienes
Apretaba el héroe su abrigo escarlata chorreado de esperma
La excitación le besaba los pies
Las botas / el olor a 1 destino presentido en fulgurantes
                    viajes de chemo
            ¡Aaarrrggghhh!
La leona parisina paría 1 cagarruta más de leyenda
                 & de tedio
Pero la sed / el irresistible imán del deseo de más miel
                    encendida /
empujaba a nuestro Lord Jim Catacumbas a arrancarse
                    las barbas
a correr persiguiendo el coño de 1 ángel que sólo a él le huía

Saint John of the Cross Gives Neal Cassady a Lift / on the Border between Myth & Dream

The highway bends toward the center of its own
centrifugal fire
Tijuana vanishes floating beneath the brains of the eye
Shards of cabaret & mattress push the wake
of fairies that impregnates the illusion of this moment
On the radio: Jim Morrison swallows spores sprouted
on the scar of the deluge
This mental bridge takes flight
Star-filled without & within
The jungle a green speck of ganja
Destiny rolling
All of being even on stilts spits UFOs embroidered
with wings of the craziest fireflies
It is nighttime/ & on the highway / & flying
The Doors make reality their voltage with their teeth
The body of the soul bathes itself in the trip
The center curves
The curve is wild
The highway is God himself
Each ganglion / each piece
slips: is blurred
The foot braces itself
The mind weeds out euphoria from the echo
The sleepwalking assassin crossed the portals of the empty nightmare
It snowed on that stupefying night of April
The garbage strike went all the way up to his temples
The hero clutched his scarlet coat splattered with sperm
The arousal kissed his feet
His boots / the smell of a destiny foreseen in stunning bright
trips of a junkie
Aaarrrggghhh!
The Parisian lioness birthed 1 shit pellet more of legend
& of tedium
But thirst / the irresistible magnet of the desire for more
flaming honey /
pushed our Lord Jim Catacombs to pull out
his whiskers
to run in pursuit of the cunt of an angel who fled only from him

((De Chirico observaba como ojo de torre brotado sin reglas))
El asesino sonámbulo se sentó sobre el puente volado
                              del Metro Passy
El frío le abría las entrañas / la atarjea que unía la caída
de 1 sueño al torrente imparable de otro *speed* de *hashish*
Esa noche la Comuna era masacrada para todos los tiempos
El burdel se pudría con singular sinsentido
¡Lo más lejos del río!: garabateó afónico lo que quedaba
                                        de instinto
El asesino / desnudo / ensayaba piruetas
arrastrando a tajadas los carambanos manchados
                        de su abrigo-bandera
Su navaja era el cielo que renunciaba a ser cielo
La nieve: la víctima
1 crucifixión sin raíces poblaba los vagones suspendidos
                                  en la memoria
del clochard revoltoso que asaltaba esa noche la historia
                        perdida del Metro Passy
Tachadas la *pe* / la *a* / la doble *ese* / la *y* griega
Con golpes de vidrio la estación fué bautizada como
                              Metro Landrú
1 botellazo de *Viuda* / 2 oraciones en turco
Mi palacio es de vértebras / mi río Sena de orín:
Ya sin aspas el mundo
En santa paz la carroña.

((De Chirico observed it as being the tower's eye bursting forth unruly))
The sleepwalking assassin sat down on the flying bridge
                              of the Passy Metro
The cold opened up his entrails / the sewer pipe that united the fall
of 1 dream to the unstoppable torrent of another *speed* of *hashish*
That night the Commune was massacred for all time
The bordello rotted away with singular senselessness
The farthest away from the river!: he voicelessly scribbled what remained
                              of instinct
The assassin / naked / essayed pirouettes
dragging piece by piece the stained icicles
                    of his coat-flag
His razor was the sky that renounced being heaven
The snow: the victim
A rootless crucifixion populated the wagons suspended
                              in memory
of the rebellious clochard who that night assaulted the lost
                    history of the Passy Metro
The crossed out *P* / the *A* / the double *S* / and the *Y*
With blows of glass the station was christened as
                              Landrú Metro
1 blow of a *Widow's* bottle / 2 prayers in Turkish
My palace is made of vertebrae / my river Seine of urine:
The world now without crosses & exes
The carrion in sainted peace.

Retrato de memoria de mi padre Jack Kerouac / desde esta estación del universo

Sus aletas de delfín no son voluminosas ni visibles
pero qué vuelo de arpón el de su risa
& cómo rompe termómetros su llanto
Si el mar : su irrenunciable mar
pierde carne / carne & uñas
la carretera-garganta sin fin de sus húmedos instintos
emborracha con la dulzura
con la que 1 niño aprieta explora
bautiza por primera vez su nebulosa
Desnudez que llueve truena rehiletea olas
reinventando lo que antes sólo se llamaba
labio o sólo beso o sólo viento
viento de viento / trabalenguas que se pellizcaba solo
Sin 1 sólo salto sorpresa
en el radar o en la brújula encharcada
de este ser balsa & fauno
nervio & cosquilla remanervios
Contagioso-íntegro-febril acercapájaros
al que yo le dedico —entre destellos—
estos rayos de luz-bragueta abierta
la escultura de amor
yegua ardiente de jadeos
Ángel subterráneo
que hace sudar al pacto interno que frota esta canción

Portrait from Memory of my Father Jack Kerouac / from this Station of the Universe

His dolphin's fins are neither voluminous nor visible
but what a harpoon's flight is his laughter
& how thermometers burst at his weeping
If the sea : his irrenounceable sea
loses flesh / flesh & nails
the endless highway-maw of his humid instincts
gets drunk on the sweetness
with which a child clutches explores
christens for the first time his nebulous
Nakedness that rains thunders spins waves
reinventing that which before was merely called
lip or merely kiss or merely wind
wind of wind / tonguetangler that only pinched
Without a single startled jump
on radar or on the waterlogged compass
of this raft & faun
nerve & nervebranch-tickling being
Contagious-integral-febrile bird charmer
to whom I dedicate —amid bright flashes—
these rays of light-open fly
the sculpture of love
mare horse burning with gasps
Subterranean angel
who makes sweat the inner pact that lewdly rubs this song

Carta abierta a Kenneth Rexroth

Sin 1 tornado que enarene su garganta
este planeta gime / ayuno de jardines & asideros
La nieve enlodada : los párpados vencidos
Tam-tams de Áfricas internas
no han logrado trocar su peste en rosas
su humareda enemiga de fragancias
en suaves remolinos / donde sólo la bruja chispa del deseo alumbre & se desmande
Las cabras & los toros arrancados de su cielo
piden limosna en dispensarios / mataderos / mercados de forraje
bailarinas ves llorando / congeladas /
tragafuegos dibujándose en sus ingles
mares de pie & asfaltos de no entienden
comedores de plátanos con playeras que dicen: *Hegel vitamínico*
& 1000 & 1 atrocidades
con su talco coagulado / como único bolsillo
Si la materia fuera cíclope
éste no sería su ojo
Gorila destronado
Nereida ya marchita
Horca resucitándose
para mejor burlarse de sus propias células colgadas
Calistenia trágica de paracaídas atorados
Bajo 1 lluvia de excrementos
/ mezcla de catsup e intestinos de gorrión /
que no puede detener ni siquiera 1 sortilegio de gitana

Open Letter to Kenneth Rexroth

Without a tornado to fill your throat with sand
this planet whines / a fast of gardens & handholds
The mud-laden snow : defeated lids of eyes
Tom-toms of internal Africas
have not managed to change your stench into roses
your smoky enemy fragrances
into soft whirlwinds / where only the witch spark of desire flashes & rampages
The she-goats & bulls plucked from your heaven
beg alms in dispensaries / slaughter houses / feed markets
you see ballerinas weeping / frozen /
fire eaters sketching themselves on your groin
oceans standing erect & asphalt of incomprehension
banana eaters with t-shirts that say: *Hegel vitamins*
& 1000 & 1 atrocities
with their clotted talcum / like a solitary pocket
If the material world were a cyclops
this would not be its eye
Dethroned gorilla
Nereid now wrinkled & withered
A gallows reviving itself
the better to mock its own hung cells
Tragic calisthenics of unopening parachutes
Beneath a rain of excrements
/ mixture of catsup & sparrow intestines /
that cannot even put a stop to a gypsy woman's spell

Demasiado viejo para seguir rocanroleando, demasiado joven para morir

(monólogo interior a propósito de la poesía de Richard Brautigan)

Si tocara la armónica como Bob Dylan
si silbara a brincos como en los tiempos de Hammelin
o viviera en el interior de 1 queso gruyere
no lo haría mucho mejor.
Allen, Gregory, Gary, Michael
la vieja tribu beat en coro le cantan aquello de *dónde acaba tu cuerpo y*
dónde empieza el mío
los Pop de Liverpool le retan a componerle una balada a la espuma de una cerveza
Allen Jones enloquece con las pecas de Marcia (nuevas teorías &
aventuras cromáticas nacen a partir de esto).
Sus libros más que hermosos son 1 morral de sorpresas
donde el amor habla de la libido a la vez que aplaude
como un tenedor frotándose con 1 cuchara & 1 cuchillo.
Demasiado viejo para seguir rocanroleando
demasiado joven para morir
John Giorno, Erica Jong, Eduard Sanders, Frank Lima, Tom Veitch
⠀⠀le escriben cartas de amor
⠀⠀le mandan por correo *sandwichs* de salami
S.O.S. que Richard contesta soltando globos cada que pasa por los parques
Como 1 niño que aboliera la pornografía con sus travesuras encueradas,
con su pasión por el sistema Braille
(Mi ojo dice sí
pidiéndole solidaridad a mis pestañas.)
Podría cantar mil anécdotas de Claudia Sol dispuesta a treparse
en su nave espacial rumbo a la galaxia de Richard Brautigan
Si bailara en 1 trapecio
al ritmo de psilocibina de sus venas droguis
no lo haría mucho mejor
1 de esos besos hace trampa (Bum!) & se desparrama con la carga
de 10 besos normales
Berkeley, Woodstock (en esencia, no en su anécdota) estallan todavía
entre los cabellos de la gente que se acerca cada vez más a la electricidad de
los mamíferos lumínicos
otra ética estética
otra sensibilidad
Fuego & lluvia como requintearon las cuerdas vocales de James Taylor

Too Old to Keep On Rock & Rolling, Too Young to Die

(Interior monologue regarding the poetry of Richard Brautigan[27])

If he had played the harmonica like Bob Dylan
if he had piped & skipped about as in the days of Hamelin
or lived inside a gruyère cheese
he couldn't have done much better.
Allen, Gregory, Gary, Michael
the old beat tribe in chorus sings him the one that goes *where your body ends &*
where mine begins
the Pop musicians of Liverpool dare him to compose a ballad to the foamy head of a
    beer
Allen Jones goes crazy over Marcia's freckles (new theories &
chromatic adventures are born out of this).
His more than beautiful books are a satchel full of surprises
in which love speaks of libido as it applauds
like a fork rubbing up against a spoon & a knife.
    Too old to keep on rock & rolling
    too young to die
John Giorno, Erica Jong, Eduard Sanders, Frank Lima, Tom Veitch
    they write him love letters
    they send him salami sandwiches in the mail
That is why Richard answers by setting balloons free each time he passes through
    parks
Like a child who would abolish pornography with his buck naked pranks,
with his passion for the Braille system
(My eye says yes
begging my lashes for solidarity.)
He could sing a thousand anecdotes about Claudia Sol ready to climb aboard
his space ship on its way to the Richard Brautigan Galaxy
If he had danced on a trapeze
to the psilocybin rhythm of his drugged out veins
he couldn't have done much better
1 of those kisses sets a trap (Boom!) & lets off a charge
equal to 10 normal kisses
Berkeley, Woodstock (in essence, not in his anecdote) are still exploding
in the of hair of the people who approach more & more the electricity of
light-producing mammals
another esthetic ethics
another sensibility

¿Qué esto no es 1 nota literaria? (¿dónde viven arqueólogos llorones?)

1 colilla de cigarro
1 rock sabor de zarzamora
1 noche acostado con las luces de neón
no tartamudean como el alfabeto Morse de las notas literarias
Decir que tiene 41 años
que es pecoso como 3 guayabas
que nació en esta ciudad interglacial nos lo revelan tan poco como la radiografía o el
     electroencefalograma
a la hora de poner en claro la taquicardia, la adrenalina de estos tiempos
(¿Qué más para que revienten de satisfechos los curiosos?) Vive en Pasadena.
Su amor por los delfines 1 un día de estos lo vuelve 1 hombre rana
El Desamor, la rigidez, la diplomacia; la antisensibilidad de los fotógrafos
lo odian *bien en serio*
Él ríe
pero no los deja vivos
no los deja vivos
Quien lo confunda con 1 escritor de oficio, de status, está inscribiendo su diarrea
en 1 casilla que no le corresponde (sic / sic).

Fire & rain just like James Taylor's vocal chords riffed

Is this not a literary note? (where do the bawling archeologists live?)

A cigar butt
a blackberry flavored rock
a night in bed with neon lights
do not stutter like the Morse code of literary notes
To say that he is 41 years old
that he is as freckled as 3 guayabas
that he was born in this interglacial city reveals to us as little as does radiography or
    an electroencephalogram
at the hour of making the tachycardia obvious, the adrenaline of those times
(What more to make the curious burst with satisfaction?) He lives in Pasadena.
His love for dolphins : one of these days he will turn into a frog man
The Lack of Affection, the rigidity, the diplomacy, the anti-sensibility of the
    photographers
they *really seriously* hate him
He laughs
but he will not leave them alive
he will not let them live.
He who would mistake him for a writer by profession, of status, is checking off, using
    diarrhea
a box that does not apply (sic / sic).

Abisinia's Shock

¡1 carga de oro para el aguilucho Rimbaud!
150 táleros : pieza x pieza :
¿Qué querrá decir este viento de aves / anestesiada la tarde?
Tanta vagancia & pasión ¿qué querrán decir?
Este texto brotado del túnel ansía dibujarlo
:: Adolescente espectral / feto prodigio
Camellero del limbo / Negación & vaivén ::
Sí, el poeta es realmente 1 ladrón de fuego
¿Qué ha pasado ¡carajo! del *Vuelve, vuelve Verlaine*
                    al marfil / las caravanas / la costa?
Los fantasiosos los bohemios los talentos los muertos
& los imbéciles le calentaron la videncia hasta el mástil
        & el ángel se largó a reencontrarse
        ((& se arrojó de lleno))
        Ayer / si mal no recuerdo

Abyssinia's Shock

1 load of gold for Rimbaud the young eagle!

150 thalers : piece by piece :

What can this wind of fowls mean / the evening anesthetized?

Such indolence & passion : What can it mean?

This text burst out from the tunnel anxiety to describe him

:: Spectral adolescent / prodigious freak

Camel driver of limbo / Negation & coming & going ::

Yes, the poet is really a thief of fire

What has become : Fucking hell! of the *Come back, come back Verlaine*

to the ivory / the caravans / the coast?

The dream peddlers the bohemians the talents the dead

& the imbeciles heated his clairvoyance to the topmast

& the angel went off to meet him again

((& hurled himself with full force))

Yesterday / if I am not mistaken

Escudo de crin : Brazos de cristal

A la memoria de Juan Nicolás Arturo Rimbaud

¡Con cuántos pelones o greñudos no te han confundido!
A las orillas de tus propios vértices
Desafiando la visión erecta de tu sombra
/ Saliva bailando entre los dientes /

Todos quisimos ser ese niño
que enlodaba de misterio a los escribas

Impulso insensato e infinito hacia los esplendores invisibles
¡Las voces reconstituidas; el despertar fraterno de todas las energías corales & orquestales
& sus aplicaciones instantáneas; la ocasión, única, de liberar nuestros sentidos!

Después del Diluvio no has vuelto
Juan Nicolás Arturo

Tu homosexualismo era panteísta & al revés
El solo nombre de Verlaine significa absolutamente todo esto
Tu definitivo amor al cosmos
:: Sus milagros / sus desastres
su fortuna / su peligro ::
Pero el cuerpo es 1 tesoro que prodigar
& tú lo hiciste
Culeaste con los soles de la Psyche
Penetraste a la Diosa misma en su capullo
Cabrón tan esperma / tan óvulo
      Única flor hermafrodita
      Te beso & te extraño
      Carnal de mi tormenta
      mi embriaguez & mis heridas

Horsehair Shield : Arms of Glass

To the memory of Jean Nicolas Arthur Rimbaud

They have confused you with so many bald or shaggy haired men!
At the edges of your own vertexes
Defying the erect vision of your shadow
/ Saliva dancing between your teeth /

We all wanted to be that boy
who muddied the scribes with mystery

Insensate & infinite impulse toward the invisible splendors
The reconstituted voices, the fraternal awakening of all the choral & orchestral energies
& their instantaneous application; the one & only chance to liberate our senses!

After the Deluge you have not returned
Jean Nicolas Arthur

Your homosexualism was pantheistic & in reverse
The mere name of Verlaine signifies all of this absolutely
Your definitive love of the cosmos
:: His miracles / his disasters
his fortune / his danger ::
But the body is a treasure to squander
& you did that
You butt fucked the suns of Psyche
You penetrated the pussy of the Goddess herself
You son of a bitch with so much sperm / so much ovum
            One & only hermaphrodite flower
            I kiss you & I long for you
            Carnal[28] of my torment
            my drunkenness & my wounds

El loco de Pound ha venido a verme

El loco de Pound ha venido a verme
Desde nuestro primer encuentro Dioses & Diosas devoraban sus propios gusanos
Se vivía poesía / perseguidos por rayos
& en pleno reino de las camisas de fuerza
Nosotros volábamos
(Nomás al soñarnos)
Saint Elizabeth sigue llagando pellejos & almas
¡Te manda besos la Anne Sexton!

Crazy Pound Has Come to See Me

Crazy Pound has come to see me
Since our first encounter Gods & Goddesses have devoured their own worms
He lived poetry / pursued by lightning bolts
& under the reign of straitjackets
The two of us would fly
(Only when dreaming of each other)
Saint Elizabeth[29] keeps on wounding hides & souls
Anne Sexton sends you kisses!

Bataille reencarnado

A la memoria de William Burroughs

Sediento de arder
Ignorándolo todo
Coágulo de sangre que crece & se desborda
Desnudez de la suerte
Peste encarnada
Herida incurable del ser
De pie / en 1 tren repleto
Con el corazón golpeante la muerte entra
Se disloca en el absurdo
En el vacío abierto al desorden
Aleluya de los sentidos
¡La voluptuosidad exige fiebre!
Tirar por la ventana todo lo que hay
Arrodillado en la boca de la noche en que se pudren las costras humanas
Lo que no podemos tocar sin disolvernos
Emperrado en la acción sin tregua
Obsesionado con gozar
Qué podría yo si la sangre me corriese de los ojos
Haciendo círculos
Apareciendo / desapareciendo
Ignorando quién soy
Salvo que me embriago & que embriago
Más allá de la poesía las ratas roen
Locamente / sin retorno
Siempre en juego
En estado de gracia
Flecha lanzada sin cesar
A contracorriente
Cara a cara a la muerte más loca & más ansiosa
De cerca / de lejos
Convulsivamente
¿Mi voz?
:: Desgarradora ::

Bataille Reincarnate

To the memory of William Burroughs

Thirsty from burning
Unaware of everything
Curdling of blood that increases & overflows
Nakedness of fortune
Plague incarnate
Incurable wound of being
Standing / in a crowded train
With a pounding heart death enters
It becomes dislocated in the absurd
In the void open to disorder
The hallelujah of the senses
Voluptuousness demands fever!
Throw all that there is out the window
Kneeling in the mouth of the night where the human scabs putrefy
That which we cannot touch without melting away
Stubbornly persisting in the action without truce
Obsessed with delight
What could I do if the blood flowed from my eyes
Going in circles
Appearing / disappearing
Unaware of who I am
Save that I get drunk & that I make others drunk
Far beyond poetry the rats gnaw away
Madly / with no coming back
Always at play
In a state of grace
The arrow launched ceaselessly
Against the current
Face to face with the maddest & most anxious death
Up close / from afar
Convulsively
My voice?
:: Heart rending ::

Mallarmé asaltado

Faunos ebrios del trasmundo
Desafíos desgarrados
Diversos amigos míos
He aquí roída mi nativa nobleza
De las barbas de las calles cuelgan cantos
joyas lúgubres asaeteadas por el hambre
/ pus & sombras : sed vacía /
Encanecen los drenajes
las jaurías se autoapañan
Hablo en oro & me desgasto
Flor extraña la del sueño por las noches
Cuerno recio : borbotón de sangre
Las arenas de polilla vueltas tótems
por la angosta boca abierta de la herida
No estoy muerto
Pulso mi arco
La humareda cojimanca del paisaje hace buches de rodillas
No hay cristales que galopen de mi mente a esa banqueta
De mis luces / sólo espinas
pero no / pero no

Mallarmé Assaulted

Drunken fauns from the hidden world
Defiances clawed apart
Diverse friends of mine
Behold my innate nobility gnawed away
From the beards of the streets hang cantos
lugubrious jewels beset by hunger
/ pus & shadows : empty thirst /
The drains go gray
the packs of wild dogs repair themselves
I speak in gold & wear myself out
Strange flower of night dreaming
Harsh horn : gushing of blood
Moth dust made into totems
by the narrow open mouth of the wound
I am not dead
I pluck my bow
The lame-limbed smokiness of the landscape makes maws out of knees
There are no crystals that gallop from my mind to that curb
Of my lights / only thorns
but no / but no

William Shakespeare llega a Chilpancingo

William Shakespeare llega a Chilpancingo
casi rompiéndose la cresta
en 1 accidente de avioneta

1 tejón (de los sonámbulos)
lo mira con sigilo

1 federal de seguridad
le tira & no le atina

William Shakespeare llega (como quiere)
la cadera aún caliente & olorosa
el cráneo invadido de llameantes salamandras
encajadas como almohadas de roca & musgo

William Shakespeare se pierde en Chilpancingo
—del cabaret al ginecólogo—
viaja ya parado de puntas
ya besando la quijada de su antilecumberri paulatino
su sangre-túnel
su helicóptero-espinazo
su brujísima voluntad
el capricho en vuelo
sobre el que monta & pare exclamaciones en su huida

William Shakespeare / que sembró su maceta de viruelanegra en Chilpancingo
excursión en camino real
intoxicación que ahora paladeamos como clásica
William Shakespeare ajedreceando en Chilpancingo

William Shakespeare Arrives in Chilpancingo[30]

William Shakespeare arrives in Chilpancingo
almost breaking his crown
in a small plane accident

A Jehovah's Witness[31] (of the sleepwalking kind)
watches him on the sly

a federal security officer
shoots at him & does not hit him

William Shakespeare arrives (as he likes it)
his hip still hot & fragrant
his cranium invaded by flaming salamanders
fit together like pillows of rock & moss

William Shakespeare gets lost in Chilpancingo
—on the way from the cabaret to the gynecologist—
traveling now on tip-toe
now kissing the jaw of his anti-Lecumberri[32] gradual progress
his blood-tunnel
his helicopter backbone
his most witch-like will
his caprice in flight
upon which he rides & lets out cries while fleeing

William Shakespeare / who seeded his flowerbed with black small pox in
    Chilpancingo
excursion on the camino real
intoxication that we now savor as classic
William Shakespeare playing chess in Chilpancingo

¡Salud!

Calavera Antonin
carnal de mi alma
Escribirte qué trampa
Es 1 saludo
& beso-charrasca
buceando profundo
en tu manantial-piel cargada
: Tu psiquis: tu gesto :
Abuelo de karmas
Tawerí de mi errancia
Como nube que aprieta tu iluminada quijada
hoy te hablo / te danzo
te flecho peregrino
flor a flor en tu cactus
Esta carta / este canto
que debió escribirte Anaïs Nin
para que supiera el descaro torrente
de pedorrearse 1 *Te amo*
De Rodez a mi chantre
de tu magia a mi espacio
Te la unto / me embarco
fuera de las campiñas & las jaulas francesas
En la entraña más lumpen
te beso / mi doble
en lo alto de 1 cielo sin horas de escape
Calavera-carnal
no te he dicho ni 1 *¡Suave!*
ni 1 *¡cámara / compa!* / ni 1 *¡vente a embriagarte!*
El sol-camarón
se tuesta en mis sienes
Ni 1 solo electroshock con sus garfios
ha pisado esta *chambre*
Paséate & danza
Dinamita esta casa de geishas malcriadas
El jardín de 1 poeta es magma de abejas
Calavera-carnal
Aguijón de mi alma

Here's Looking at You!

Antonin skull & bones
carnal[33] of my soul
Writing you is such a scam
This is a greeting
& knife cutting kiss
delving deeply
into your charged fountainhead skin
: Your spirit: your gesture :
Grandfather of karmas
Tawerí of my rootless wandering
Like a cloud that presses your enlightened jaw
Now I speak you / I dance you
I arrow you pilgrim
flower to flower on your cactus
This letter / this canto
that Anaïs Nin should have written you
so as to know the insolent torrential
flatulence of 1 *I love you*
From Rodez to my temple cantor
from your magic to my space
I anoint you / I embark
out of the green fields & jails of France
In the most lumpen entrails
I kiss you / my double
at the peak of 1 heaven with no time to escape
Carnal skull & bones
I have never told you a single *Suave!*
or *Right on!* / *Compadre!* / or a *Let's get drunk*!
The sun sea prawn
is scorched on my temples
& not even one electroshock with its hooks
has entered this *chambre*
Come on in & dance
This house of ill-mannered geishas is dynamite
The garden of a poet is a magma of bees
Carnal skull & bones
Goading sting of my soul

Leopoldo María

Afilada, fálica, furiosa faz
Malcolm Lowry

Jeringa sobre cráter
La mirada desviada
El greñero sin control
Mi paisaje es siempre
algo que cerca hipnotiza & avasalla
El fantasma del tufo exterior
disfrazado de caramelo interno
1 convulsión refrigerada
que se vuelve realidad
El avión se rompió
Se quemó mi conciencia
Pestes del sueño detenerme a escribir
Aullar / gemir / chupar
Mi chamarra es mi pellejo
mi pedazo de jerga
mi espejo de lidia
Ya todo vacío & en derrumbe
& no precisamente mudas estas puntuales ratas
que roen el humo transparente de mi hojalata verde
Humus hubo / hay & habrá
Ya ni sudo ni río
Derribo a veces bichos
Otras / noches / soy su plato
La música agujerea siempre
Vuelve real lo velado
Bañada la luna en sangre
Los libros son pura máscara
La rana se convierte en príncipe
En oro la selva negra
Mejor este cuchillo cierto
Esta escultura de pólvora
Este hedor *increscendo*
/ Hocico con hocico /
Vivir me costó la vibra
Adentrarme la esperanza
Lo dice mi culo al sentir la bruma
Este sueño es gris
Yo soy su lápida

Leopoldo María[34]

> Sharpened, phallic, furious face
> *Malcolm Lowry*

Syringe above a crater
My gaze askance
My wild unkempt hair
My landscape is always
something that encloses hypnotizes & enslaves
The ghost of the exterior stink
disguised as a sweetmeat within
a refrigerated convulsion
that becomes reality
The aircraft was torn apart
My consciousness burned
Dream plagues keeping me from writing
Howling / groaning / sucking
My jacket is my hide
my piece of jargon
my mirror of combat
Now all is empty & in collapse
& not exactly mute are these punctual rats
that gnaw the transparent smoke of my green tinplating
Humus there was / is & will be
I now neither sweat nor laugh
At times I squash bugs
Other / nights / I am their meal
The music always pierces through
The veiled becomes real
The moon bathed in blood
Books are simply a mask
The frog changes into a prince
The black jungle into gold
Better this undeniable knife
This gunpowder sculpture
This fetid odor *in crescendo*
/ I root about with my snout /
Living has cost me my vibe
Let hope enter me
Says my ass upon sensing the thick mist
This dream is grey
I am its tombstone

Única sangre

Para Rebeca López

Naciste del semen de Gerard de Nerval
Exactamente a las plantas de su horca
De sus ojos radiantes / destrozados
De la entraña de su videncia inmaculada
De su poderosa mente extraterrena
De su charrasqueado & singular destino
Brotaste / buscándome
Enfrentando los océanos imposibles
Librando el albedrío de las tormentas
/ Como fuera /
Con tal de llegar a besar todas mis llagas
A los pies alados de esa misma horca
De la que también soy hijo

One Blood

For Rebecca López[35]

You were born of the semen of Gerard de Nerval
Precisely at the base of his gallows
From his radiant / ruined eyes
From the entrails of his immaculate clairvoyance
From his powerful otherworldly mind
From his knife-scarred & singular destiny
You burst forth / looking for me
Confronting the impossible oceans
Setting loose the free will of the storms
/ As it were /
In order to kiss all my wounds & sores
At the winged feet of that same gallows
From which I too was born.

Para El J.C.

Ahijado puerperal de la Ciudad Luz
Caleidoscopio arlequín de sus espectros
Brujo tallado en sus bosques & empedrados
Clochard cosido para el fin de los tiempos a la flor de esa coraza
Oficio en silencio
Esta misa quebradita
Porque sí / porque los Doors
Bajo la hoguera de la ojiva de los puentes
Donde la Maga me va a regalar hoy el resplandor del s-o-l

For El J.C.[36]

Innate godson of the City of Light
Kaleidoscope harlequin of its specters
Sculpted sorcerer-warlock in its woody parks & cobbled streets
Clochard sewn to the flower of that shield till the end of time
Divine office in silence
This wild cumbia mass
Just because / because the Doors
Under the bonfire of the steep arch of the bridges
Where la Maga[37] will today gift me the splendor of the s-u-n

Visiones de la Rue Morgue

Para Samuel Beckett

Gajo a gajo
la sangre de la luz es 1 coro de peces
que interrumpe la locura de la noche oscura
Todo lo que existe / quieto
En sus escalas & en sus púas quieto
Rasgados rabos & hocicos
falangetas & cochambres
1 foco
–cráneo reducido del obeso Francis Bacon–
oficia entre cortocircuitos & centellas
Pomos & pulmones derramados
Toda el agua bautismal
que pide a gritos el ansia vertebral de 1 feto
/ 1 grito-cascada bebiendo la caricia del silencio /
Todo el orbe pateado por la ebria ceguera de Dios mismo
Esta música de siempre / enredada al corazón del tiempo /
:: Movemos & hundimos las patitas ::
Son de sueños las gradas del ostión
Al filo en que a sus babas les da lo mismo
castrar a la luz / masturbar a su sombra
enterrarse mudas / en cualquier rampa de arena o ilusión

Visions of the Rue Morgue

For Samuel Beckett

Sliver by sliver
the blood of the light is a chorus of fish
that interrupts the madness of the dark night
All that exists / is still
In its scales & in its spiky quills still
Ragged tails & snouts
wedge-shaped & pig-filthy
A lightbulb
—reduced cranium of the obese Francis Bacon—
officiates between short-circuits & sparking embers
Doorknobs & lungs scattered
All of the baptismal water
begged for with screams by the vertebral yearning of a fetus
/ a scream-cascade drinking the caress of silence /
The entire globe kicked in drunken blindness by God himself
This same music as always / entangled in the heart of time /
:: We move & submerge our little feet ::
The terraced beds of oysters are a thing of dreams
To the point that it is all the same to his drooling slugs
to castrate the light / to masturbate to his shadow
to bury themselves mutely / in any slope of sand or illusion

Comencemos / con las arboledas de la sangre

Carnavalito tlaxcalteca de Lou Reed
Lentes de desolación & córnea blanda
Lentes-piscina de licor barato
Lentes-cementerio de chinches & bostezos de albatros
Chamarrita parpadeante de hemorragias malcosidas
Pantalones casi bolsas donde el cloroformo sostiene apenas sus quijadas
Quién eres sino el gemido & el sudor con que montas a tu sombra
Hablas mucho sí de los huecos los hoyitos (alcantarillas encueradas)
Donde dices —al derecho & al revés— que le haces el amor a tus cigarros
Sería lindo (vamos pues) golpeadoramente necesario
Que la nieve te llegara 1 día de visita
& desparramara sus pastillas sus abrigos en tus milpas
(1 lágrima de Gershwin
1 cantito de viejas varicosas
1 uña sin latidos de algún mudo cirquero jubilado)
Que la nieve se posara
Como manos de anillos ya sin miedo
Hasta el fondo de tus ojos
Que ahora cubres / que ahora ocultas
Con venditas de química aridísima
& boletos de excursiones recto abajo de tus sueños
Otro blues otro trago nos cantara
Carnalito tlaxcalteca
Cabroncete mitotero / Espartaco-sacarracas

We Commence / with the Trees of Blood

Lou Reed's little Tlaxcalteca[38] carnival
Eyeglasses of desolation & soft cornea
Poolside-eyeglasses of cheap liquor
Cemetery-eyeglasses of bedbugs & albatross yawns
Small blinking jacket of badly sewn hemorrhages
Pants almost purses in which chloroform barely holds up its jaws
Who are you but the whining moan & the sweat with which you ride your shadow
You certainly talk a lot about the hollows, the little holes (stark naked sewers)
In which you swear —up & down— that you make love to your cigars
It would be beautiful (let's have it, then) strikingly necessary
That the snow come pay you a visit some day
& scatter its pills its coats in your corn fields
(1 Gershwin tear
1 little song about varicose old ladies
1 finger nail without the pulse of some mute retired circus ring master)
May the snow fall
Like now fearless ring-laden hands
Up to the depth of your eyes
That you now cover / that you now hide
With bandages of the most arid chemistry
& tickets to excursions directly beneath your dreams
Another blues song another shot of booze to sing to us
My carnalito Tlaxcalteca
Rowdy dear bastard / Needle-sharing Spartacus

Monte de Venus

Monte de Venus
pequeño / precioso
–hagámosle fiestas–
Sueño del sueño de esta vida-sueño
Gema rocosa junto al manantial
Le canto & deseo
Lo baño de sombras
Lo beso extasiado
Bajo él / 1 hembra
las puertas del cielo
la vid de la música
las playas del sexo
No hay cristal más rotundo
Robarse el vellocino es esto
Derramarse en los trópicos
Revolotear los trasmundos
Con el pájaro en alto
Agotar la sed sacra
La obsesión que nos crece
desde antiguos capullos

Mount de Venus

Monte de Venus
small / precious
—let us celebrate you—
Dream of the dream of this dream-life
Rocky gem adjoined to the fountainhead
I sing & desire you
I bathe it in shadows
I kiss it ecstatically
Beneath it / a female
the gates of heaven
the grapevine of music
the shores of sex
There is no crystal more potent
This is to steal the fleece
To spill over into the tropics
To hover above the hidden worlds
With the bird on high
To quench the sacred thirst
The obsession that breeds us
from ancient buds of flowers

Jeta de santo

Carreteras de desnudez
arenas en las que mi inteligencia
no se había desollado antes
estas páginas
tantas noches mi hospital
& tantas mi balneario
El único peine al que le doy la bienvenida
Beso al que llamo de cariño: mi guadaña
Cicatriz que me persigue con sus dientes
Flor de carne que desde mis tripas corto
Única alcantarilla donde sorbo & soy sorbido
Útero aéreo que me jala por las alas
Pentagrama terroso / gruta azul
en la que vibro como nieve acorralada
El ojo velocípedo que soy
la roca pasional que me contiene / habla
Sinaí en llamas que cruza en largos zancos mi reposo
Sintaxis que se hace llamar por sus cuates: *Remolino*
Tromba hoy herida
Bombardeada por quirófanos
& densos polvos suspensivos
Piedras sin espinazo de mi yo
Allegro-cantábile de hornos
Edificios de humedad en el desierto
que surgen de este mar-infierno helado
frescos : transparentes : innegables
como una motoneta jineteada por 1 ballet travesti de sirenas
Velodenovia para la respiración del universo
Mi más querida flor recién nacida

Cheeky Mug of a Saint

Highways of nakedness
sands on which my intelligence
had not been flayed before
these pages
so many nights my hospital
& many my sanitarium
The only dragnet I welcome
I kiss whom I call with affection: my reaper
Scar that pursues me with its teeth
Flower of flesh that I cut from my guts
One & only sewer from which I suck & am sucked up by
Flying uterus that hauls me by the wings
Mud-caked pentagram / blue grotto
in which I vibrate like enclosed snow
The velocipede eye that I am
the passionate rock that contains me / speaks
Sinai in flames that my repose crosses on tall stilts
Syntax that makes one call for one's pals: *Whirlwind*
Cyclone today wounded
Bombarded by surgical theaters
& dense suspended dusts
Stones lacking the backbone of my ego
Allegro cantabile of ovens
Tall buildings of humidity in the desert
that emerge from this frozen sea-hell
fresh : transparent : irrefutable
like a motor scooter jockeyed by a transvestite mermaid ballet
Bridal veil for the breath of the universe
My most loved late-born flower

Cempazúchitl púrpura

Atreverse a escribir
en las alturas descarnadas
de esta vida
En la cima de la simia sima
/ Aventar el papalote & coronarlo
quizás signifique o no
pero derrama
Ya adentrado en gastos:
me digo / sobrevivo & sobresalto
Trapecios van & vienen
: El mío vuela firme :
sin soltar el timón de su pezón
aunque sude & llore sangre el aguacero

Purple Marigold

To dare to write
on the stark grim heights
of this life
On the summit of the simian chasm
/ Giving wind to the kite & crowning it
perhaps it means that or not
but out it spills
Now buried in expenditures:
I tell myself / I survive & I startle
Trapezes go to & fro
: Mine flies steady :
without the steering wheel coming loose from its column
though the cloudburst may sweat & weep blood

Sin embargo sobrevuelo como 1 dinastía de soles

A la memoria de Alejandra Pizarnik

¿A dónde me conduce esta escritura?
/ rosa de aspavientos: espantapájaros /
¿A qué falo de sol remojado en espuma de alabanzas?
Si no me suicido hoy / ya me suicidaré mañana
Querido amigo:
La risa en la agonía es cascada flamígera
Vivir & llagarse
llegarse / bucearse
romper el hechizo
cantar / sin piedad /
No sé
((piedra bicorne))
((vihuela rapaz))
Ni el camino de la lengua
ni las leguas a Bagdad
Odio esta *Caricatura Divina*
& en medio esta verga oscura
que llora alucinada
rompiendo todo vergel
¿La noche por siempre noche?
Es de imbécil & poeta preguntar
Comenzar por el final la quemadura
Acercarse a la ardidera
/ como ángel en su óvulo /
El infierno —llama a llama— es musical
La cola del dragón es su granalla
¿Esquirlas de la mente?
¿Alebrijes?
Estos días terrenales
han sido mi haikú / mi harakiri
¿Quién chingaos seré yo?

I Nevertheless Fly Above Like a Dynasty of Suns

In memory of Alejandra Pizarnik[39]

Where is this writing leading me?
/ rose of frenzied gestures: scarecrows /
To what sun phallus soaked in scum & praises?
If I don't kill myself today / then I will kill myself tomorrow
Dear friend:
Laughter in agony is a flamboyant waterfall
Living & wounding oneself
arriving / plunging
breaking the spell
singing / without pity /
I don't know
((two-cornered stone))
((rapacious guitar))
Neither the road of the tongue
nor the leagues to Baghdad
I hate this *Divine Caricature*
& in the midst of it all this dark cock
that weeps hallucinating
ripping apart all orchards
Is the night forever night?
It is for the imbecile & poet to ask
Commence the burning for once and for all
Get closer to the fire starter
/ like an angel inside his ovum /
Hell —from flame to flame— is musical
The tail of the dragon is his abrasive steel
Shards of the mind?
Alebrijes?[40]
These worldly days
have been my haiku / my hara-kiri
Who the fuck might I be?

Quién sino tú

Sigo vivo nada más por ti / poesía desgreñada
revólver menstruante
ronroneo escupelunas
asfalto de plasma
licuadito de semen
molcajete tiernísimo
madreadora de leyes
microbús al vacío
carterista de almas
Sólo a ti te he visto nadar en el piso
Sólo a ti te he visto rajarle el hocico a los aires
Tu mirada de atole de arroz & tamal calientito
me ha jalado imantado puesto en órbita
/ con mi boca de vértigo explorando tu clítoris púrpura /
tu voz bailadora : tus gestos de trompo
Me he graduado en tus besos de risa
En tu vientre he aprendido a deshuesar al veneno
                    & a montar mis bisontes
Ayer pantano / hoy pradera
como huazontle capeado & manglar salto en boca
                    me ha crecido el silencio
Me he arrancado la mente / he chupado sus charcos
Sus acociles : sus lirios : sus chinampas en fuga
me han secuestrado hasta el vuelo
En cada gota de mí / en cada pocillo / en cada tejita
es tu sombra solar: tu fuego avispado el rumor que se oye
la maraca el güiro el violín de entusiasmo que mi aliento
                              proyecta
milotebaldíodesuerte / elcabelloconquelazosaltolacuerda
pego la roña / tejo mis filos: mi guirnalda de puentes /
                    mi apuesta de flotantes sentidos
A toda pezuña de liebre / a todo pulmón en cubeta
& al pulso: al pulso-resorte & rentoy de todo ser-estallido
                    & todo cabalgar-fumarola.

Who But You

I remain alive only because of you / wildhaired poetry
menstruating revolver
moonspitting purring-purring
asphalt of plasma
little semen milkshake
oh so tender molcajete[41]
tiger mother of laws
minibus to the void
pickpocket of souls
Only you have I seen swim on the floor
Only you have I seen slash the snout of the winds
Your gaze of rice atole[42] & steaming hot tamal
has pulled me into orbit magnetically
/ with my mouth of vertigo exploring your purple clitoris /
your dancing voice : your spinning top faces
I have graduated in your kisses of laughter
In your belly I have learned to rid venom of its bones
                  & to mount my bison
Yesterday a swamp / today a meadow
like battered huazontle[43] & mangrove I jump in the mouth
                  I have been raised by silence
I have ripped out my mind / I have sucked up its shallow pools
Its sweet water shrimp : its water lilies : its fugitive chinampas[44]
have kidnapped me until the flight
In every drop of me / in every little bowl / in every little tile
is your solar shadow : your quick-witted fire the heard murmur
the maraca the percussion gourd the violin of enthusiasm that my breath
                             projects
myvacantlotofluck / yourhairacordwithwhichIjumprope
I hit the dirt / I weave my blades: my garland of bridges /
                  my wager of floating sensibilities
With all footspeed of a jackrabbit / with all lung force on a tray
& at the pulse: at the pulse-spring & euchre of all bursting-being
                  & all at a volcano-gallop.

Ecce homo

Caído de la nube menos proclive al estallido
Sin embargo / rebelde a ese amargo tronco
Gota a gota rana & musgo
expiación de pedruzco sin cascada
Desangro como a toro por los cuernos
el muñón resbaloso al que se aferra mi albedrío
Soy abeja africana que supera toda trampa
Dios exacto se hinca a mamarle la verga a Dios demente
Caín se le regala a Abel transformado en ajolote
                    de mirra & cempazúchitl
No habrá otro espejo más cercano a las heridas
                    de mi lengua
Soy aquél que llora
que coge lo poco que se encuentra
La caries que se chupa la mujer por no morderme
El arca de la Alianza confundida
El ala gambusina
La inabsorbible sangre
Los kilos de cerilla acumulada
tras la barda de vidrio de mi oreja anestesiada
Soy el último patio del último manicomio no dopado
Ni tengo sexo / Ni respeto a nadie
Gocé vivir
Beso a mi muerte
La empuño
la columpio
la salpico
la derrocho
No hay larva a quien no contagie de mi virus
Al miércoles de ceniza lo convierto en jueves
Porque son santos todos los balazos
Desde el primero al último.

Ecce Homo

Fallen from the cloud least inclined to explode
Nonetheless / rebellious toward that bitter trunk
Drop by drop frog & moss
atonement of rock without cascade
I bleed out like a bull through its horns
the bloody slippery stump to which my fancy clings
I am an African bee that overcomes every trap
God the precise kneels down to suck the cock of God the demented
Cain is gifted to Abel transformed into a giant salamander
                    of myrrh & marigolds
There will be no mirror closer to the wounds
                        of my tongue
I am he who weeps
who picks up what little he can find
The tooth rot the woman sucks so as not to bite me
The ark of the confounded Alliance
The store room wing
The inabsorbable blood
The kilos of accumulated match sticks
behind the glass enclosure of my anesthetized ear
I am the last courtyard of the last doped up madhouse
I have neither sex / Nor respect for anyone
I enjoyed living
I kiss my death
I grasp it with my hands
I swing it around
I spatter it
I squander it
There is no maggot who does not sicken from my virus
I change Ash Wednesday into Thursday
Because all bullet wounds are holy
From the first to the last.

Cabaret Voltaire

A la memoria de Germán Valdés

¿Buscabas yombina / tinta china?
Rompiendo lentes / retinas / teletipos
Tristan Tzara García baila tap
neuronas adentro de sus deseos dadá / paridos en la niebla
Velo jugar con el sol negro al ula ula
Cantar en el más puro remolino de gestos sordomudos
La época es su yoyo
¿Sus canicas?: Sus tanates
Cava su propio útero
Quemando el liguero del cancán en la espuma sin regreso de sus rayos infrarrojos
Ya no hay diferencia entre el pez que desova & la corriente que lo mueve
Le incendia el bote a Tongolele
Le lustra la embestida con 1 chicuelina
arrancada del saco babeante de Tin-Tan
Le deja ir sus 6 pies de gato mágico /
& de pilón la crucifica /
En el Cerro del Estribo del Placer
Poniendo a comulgar al talón con el empeine
Como 1 último homenaje a sus ancas enteógenas
/ ¡Para ver qué pasa! /

Cabaret Voltaire

In memory of Germán Valdés[45]

Were you looking for yohimbe / India ink?
Breaking lenses / retinas / teletypes
Tristan Tzara García tap dances
neurons within his dada desires / birthed in the fog
I stay awake to play hula hoop with the black sun
Singing in the purest whirlwind of deaf & dumb gestures
This era is his yoyo
His marbles?: His balls
He digs a uterus for himself
Burning the can-can garter in the no-return froth of his infra-red rays
There is now no difference between the spawning fish & the currents that move it
He sets fire to Tongolele's[46] can
He polishes the charge with a pass of his cape
pulled from Tin-Tan's[47] oozing drape shape zoot
He lets her 6 magic cat's feet depart /
& as a bonus crucifies her /
On Stirrup of Pleasure Hill
Making her heel become one with her instep
As a last homage to her entheogenic[48] rump
/ *To see what happens!* /

Desahogo

Se ictericia la tarde
el cuerpo es 1 mancha cercada de reflejos
pozo erecto en 1 Babel-ceniza
Las uvas son intestinos / el hígado: 1 higo tenso
Camino al Metro
buscando 1 centro
jugando pulsos con las visiones
—no simples fuerzas—
como si 1 ángel al seducirte / toro de fuego te desmintiera
Ah cuánta tierra : nieta de lagos
prójimos zombies pescan diarreas
1000 maniquíes te dictan cátedra
Cuarteado el ojo el sol mendigo huye pateando
La luz cual topo guarda sus pasos
Hoy leo esto / no miel de libros
hablo de grifos con 1 pegaso
Rubén se llama & es carnalito
Comemos hongos
Nos abismamos

Breathing Room

The evening yellows with jaundice
my body is a blot besieged by reflections
a two-legged pit in a Babel-of-ashes
Grapes are my intestines / my liver: a stretched taut fig
I walk to the Metro
searching for a center
wrist wrestling with visions
—not simple forces—
like an angel seducing you / a bull of fire would belie you
Ah how much land : granddaughter of lakes
neighboring zombies fish for diarrhea
1000 manikins lecture you ex cathedra
His eye cut into quarters the beggarly sun kicks & flees
The light like a mole watches over his footsteps
Today I read this / not the honey of books
I speak of griffons with a Pegasus
Rubén[49] is his name & he is my dear carnal
We eat mushrooms
We dive into the abyss

Ya lejos de la carretera

A la memoria de Infraín

> Vibraciones / vibraciones-látigo
> 1 sonido viene de la sombra / pronto
> forma 1 esfera : 1 granja : 1 grupo :
> 1 armada : 1 universo de universos
>
> *Henri Michaux*

1

Unos pantalones mugrosos & la muerte en el pecho
         ¡Órale!
Nos vemos ahí en el muro
/ pasando el vado /
los vientos cristalizándose a la izquierda
las aletas del polvo : tus aletas
1 oasis arponeándonos lo seco
En la hija de tu ojo / el cementerio
 : Mezcalito echando flores :
La Tierra & su contrario : venados silenciosos como ruidos en sus bodas
No deberías ir / pero deberías ir

2

(En esta sombra se acurruca esta rara fruta
que es el corazón del anfibio & precoz devenir infrarrealista)

Hijos de Pablo de Rokha somos
Desde antes de escribir esto / ya volábamos
Luego el continuum de lo escrito fue menos vigilado
Bailó el aliento en la punta de la lengua
Nos transfiguramos acariciando el ayayay de cada llaga
    Somos poetas
    Tam-tams del negro sol
    que nos imanta

3

Ni lumpenes ni proletarios
El pequeñodios cobrasalarios

Already Far from the Main Road

In memory of Infraín[50]

> Vibrations / vibration-whips
> a sound comes from the shadows / soon
> Forms a sphere : a barn : a group
> an armada : a universe of universes
>
> *Henri Michaux*

1

Some filthy pants & death in one's breast
          Órale![51]
We'll see each other at the wall
/ crossing the ford /
the winds crystalizing to the left
fins of dust : your fins
an oasis harpooning dry land for us
In the daughter of your eye / the cemetery
 : Peyote button shoots out flowers :
The Earth & its opposite : deer as hushed as noises in their weddings
You shouldn't go / but you must go

2

(In this shadow is nestled this rare fruit
that is the heart of the amphibious & precocious infrarealist progress)

Children of Pablo de Rokha[52] are we
Even before writing this / we were already flying
Later the continuum of the written was less monitored
Breath danced on the tip of the tongue
We transfigured ourselves caressing the ayayay of every open wound
    We are poets
    Tom-toms of the black sun
    that magnetizes us

3

Neither lumpen nor proletariat
The minor deity wage earner

ni 1 pluma rompe en los abismos nuestros
: Las auroras infras en la Casa de Usher de la araña :
Juega al balero el dulce clítoris / se embarca como a las 5 montañas en 2 cuatros
A galope tierno & crines sueltas
   Rubayat ama
         a
   Ramayana

4

Nuestra lengua ha sido púa
Es sandía / chorreante vagabunda de ancha risa
Aventura que nos ha abierto escoriaciones
Lo que éramos lo somos en el crescendo de los ecos
   A tales hombros : tales caderas
   A esos tobillos / aquellos pasos
El aprendizaje de la limpieza al escalpelo

5

...Gris es la Teoría...
Rojo el vellón de la Cannabis / La Inalámbrica

6

¿La lucha? / Contra el poder de $igno$ fari$aico$
          (Máscara vs Cabellera)
10 años después seguimos siendo Tribu
          / dondequiera lúbricos /
En Jalalpa : Minneapolis : Iquitos : Ivre Sur de Seine : Gerona :
          el Barranco & la Cañada
Perros habitados por las voces del desierto
Tlamatinimes obcecados por la flama del canto por el cuerpo
& la flama del cuerpo que es el canto
          ¡Tlacoyos de realidad!

7

El rastrojo del lenguaje no germina
si no es en hechos menguaje ya encarnado
La hazaña marabusina en tierras nahuas

does not break 1 plume in our abysses
: The daybreak infras in the spider's House of Usher :
The sweet clitoris plays at bilboquet[53] / it is boarded like the 5 mountains in 2 fours[54]
At a tender gallop & with a flowing mane
    Rubaiyat
    Loves
    Ramayana

4

Our tongue has been a sharp barb
It is a watermelon / leaking spurting vagabond of broad laughter
Adventure that has made our skin erupt
What we were we are in the crescendo of the echoes
  For such shoulders : such hips
  For those ankles / those footsteps
Training the scalpel to be clean

5

...Grey is Theory...
Red the fleece of Cannabis / The Wireless

6

The struggle? / Against the power of the Phari$aic ign
        (Mask vs Hair)
10 years later we are still a Tribe
        / lewd no matter where /
In Jalalpa : Minneapolis : Iquitos : Ivry-sur-Seine : Gerona :
       the Gully & the Ravine
Dogs haunted by the voices of the desert
Wise Tlamatinimes[55] mentally blinded by the flame of the canto through the body
& the flame of the body that is the canto
       Reality tlacoyos![56]

7

The stubble of language does not germinate
if not rooted in deeds a now incarnate dwindling
The heroic marabou deed in Nahuatl lands

–¿De a cómo la liebre lírica? / ¿con alas?
–Feliz No-Cumpleaños
El infrarrealismo no es 1 vocablo-lija
Nos han antologado nuestras noches
Cada textículo en su sitio / que bien puede ser nuestro milagro nómada

8

Es Hora Zero otra vez
Jesús Luis rasga en su luz *Canciones para gandallas*
Hay estrellas como hay ganas
hay abismos & hay caminos
Las pirañas de anteayer
son iguanas a futuro
Olas : olas : olas de sed

9

–¿Qué decían de nosotros esos empleados televisivos?
/ hijos del feliz oficio & el próspero cheque de honorarios /
–Oh Santas Risas Satánicas
–¿Ni Billy Burroughs lo sabe?
    El petate da de brincos
    / Son cocuyos en la aurora /
–¿Será eso 1 hai-kai sirio?
¿1 poeta náutico en la sierra?
¿El orgasmo del delirio?

10

Poesía-endecasilabóiler
  hermanita de Edgard Allan & Black Sabbath
caradiajos & chintreras
  qué de arrastres
    labrados en la entraña de la entraña

11

    Toco viento
: azar turgente :
Nuestra raíz está hablando

—How much for the lyrical jackrabbit? / with wings?
—A happy Un-Birthday
Infrarealism is not an abrasive term
Our nights have anthologized us
Each little text in its place / which could well be our nomad miracle

8

It is Zero Hour once again
Jesús Luis claws *Songs for Ruffians* into his light
There are stars just as there are desires
there are abysses & there are roads
The piranhas of yesteryear
are iguanas in the future
Waves : waves : waves of thirst

9

What did they say of us those television employees?
/ sons of the fortunate occupation & the prosperous check of honoraria /
—Oh Holy Satanic Laughter
—Not even Billy Burroughs knows?
       The rucksack bounces around
       / There are lightning bugs in the aurora /
—Could that be a Syrian haiku?
A nautical poet in the mountains?
The orgasm of delirium?

10

Hendecasyllaboiler poetry
   little sister of Edgar Allan & Black Sabbath
fuckfaces & screw ups
  what a lot of dredgings
    tilled in the entrails of the entrails

11

       I touch wind
: abundant chance :
Our root is speaking

/ no el enjuague del Poder & sus taquillas
sus tarifas : sus castigos : muecas cínicas : su estertor de vanidades /

12

Que Tin-Tan queme su saco
Los caminos están llenos de otros seres
        / no el cubículo ni el cargo /
Recuerda cuerpo cuanto viviste
    Cuánto evangelio de cielos abiertos
        / Subterráneamente : soberanamente /
Porque no será el miedo a ningún miedo
  el que nos haga poner a media asta
  el géiser ígneo de nuestra indignación

& este número 13 bien lo dice:
La poesía mexicana se divide en 2
la poesía mexicana & el infrarrealismo
    / Río Tula a remover /

/ not the scheming of Power & its ticket booths
its tariffs : its chastisements : cynical pouts : its noisy rales of vanities /

12

May Tin-Tan[57] *burn his zoot drapes*
The roads are full of other beings
         / not the cubicle or the job /
Remember body how much you lived
    How much gospel of the open skies
       / Subterraneously : sovereignly /
Because it won't be the fear of any other fear
   that will make us haul to half mast
   the igneous geyser of our indignation

& this number 13 says it well:
Mexican poetry is divided in 2
Mexican poetry & infrarealism
   / *Río Tula to shake things up* /

Mariana Larrosa aparece

Mariana Larrosa aparece
reciensalidita de 1 duchazo de aguamiel & canela
las banquetas sonríen / entre la excitación & la alarma
& se oye clarito clarito cómo se desbocan
multitudes de bocinas cardiacas

Mariana Larrosa aparece
& no son sus dedos / herederos de los dedos
que a diario tan malamente nos tocan

gajos de sandía son sus ojos
frescuras envueltas en sangre
si viene de la muerte o de 1 patiovecino
si viene de dormir en la nuca de 1 árbol
o de masturbarle las antenas a 1 caracol submarino
ella nos lo va a pintar-transmitir
con manzanas con juegos

Ella que se habla de tú
con las luces fantasmas / las luces traviesas
ella que sabe de splits en do agudo
& entrechats encerrados en clósets de vidrio
ella que ahora camina & se arquea
ronronea maúlla sacude sus pliegues multiplica sus vellos
electriza zaguanes pone a volar azoteas

1 rama de dátiles
cuelga entre su boca & la mía
1 columpio de gises / listos
a colorear 1000 gargantas
administraciones de hoteles
nuestros taparrabos de espuma
ORNITORRINCA MÁS BELLA NON HABÍAMOS VISTO
los antisiquiatras le chiflan
le regalan almendras le regalan huevos de boa
a ella que es la reina de los erizos salvajes
la abejarreina de las comunas anarkas
(el naipe-túnel: la apuesta-riesgo en las brasas
quemadora de posturas & reglas que sofocan a esta especie-silladerruedas

Mariana Larrosa[58] Appears

Mariana Larrosa appears
Recently emerged from a shower of honeywater & cinnamon
The sidewalks laugh / between excitement & alarm
& there is heard clearly so clearly
a multitude of heartbursting horns sounding off

Mariana Larrosa appears
& her fingers are not / the heirs of the fingers
that so badly touch us each day

watermelon slices are her eyes
fresh coolness enveloped in blood
if she comes from death or a neighboring patio
if she comes from sleeping in the crotch of a tree
or from masturbating the antennas of an underwater snail
she will paint-transmit it for us
with apples with games

She who speaks of you
with ghost lights / the mischievous lights
she who knows of splits in C sharp
& entrechats enclosed in glass closets
she who now walks & arches up
purrs meows shakes her folds multiplies her fine fur
electrifies doorways makes rooftops fly

A frond of dates
hangs between her mouth and mine
a swing of chalk / ready
to color 1000 throats
hotel administrations
our loin cloths of froth
A MORE BEAUTIFUL PLATYPUS WE HAVE NEVER SEEN
the anti-psychiatrists wolf whistle
they bestow almonds give boa eggs
to her who is the queen of the savage hedgehogs
the queenbee of the anarchist communes
(the playing card tunnel: a hazard-bet on the embers
burner of posturings & rules that stifle this wheelchair-species

croupier paranoica de los antecomedores del póker)
    ¡Pagamos por ver!

Mariana Larrosa aparece / ya lo dije: lo digo: está dicho /
con este movimiento este sudor este gesto
que tiembla se emociona sonríe / cada que sé que la veo
cada que sé que la he visto & que me niego lluviosa espermática
                             atlántidamente a dejar de mirarla
& hola & quiúbole & qué jáis (entre barandales macetas techumbres de calor
    muerdeláminas)
& hola & quiúbole/ & jamás ella & yo
vamos a andar por ahí borrando 1 grito
chorreando veneno desviando a otra esquina
al vagabundo chancito de matar nuestros viejos pellejos
respirar meteoritos —ocasionales incendios—
desnudarnos en sartenes de silencios calientes
citar a esta fiesta / al tiro al toque

que venga quien sepa
con su itacate de nervios su cantimplora de films o de sueños para pasársela rico
existan o no existan los consabidos espejos los esperados aromas
las lunasdemiel o de chicle o de calabacitas rellenas
que dicen que brotan & se vuelven presencia
llamarada colchón conversación importante
apenas cruzas de 1 brinco apenas te acercas gateando
a la espinosa frontera cercada de flechas letreros que indican
    los más cercanos hoteles para después de morir

Mariana Larrosa aparece
baterista de su propio baile
cuerda-yerbacrecida de su único e inimitable swing

paranoid card dealer of poker breakfast nooks)
    We'll pay to watch!

Mariana Larrosa appears / I have already said it: I say it: it has been said /
with this movement this sweat this gesture
she trembles gets excited smiles / I know that each time I see her
I know each time I have seen her & I refuse rainfully spermatically
                              atlantically to stop looking at her
& hello & quiúbole[59] & hi (among railings flower pots on rooftops of a maddening
    heat)
& hello & quiúbole / & never will she and I
walk along over there obliterating a scream
squirting jets of venom detouring to another street corner
on the slight vagabond chance of doing away with our old hides
breathing in meteorites —occasional fires—
getting naked in skillets of hot silences
citing this fiesta / straight away right now

who knows what may pass
with her leftovers of nerves her hip flask of films or dreams to have a good time
they exist or they do not those well-known mirrors hoped-for aromas
the honeymoons or gum moons or stuffed squash moons
that they say spring up & become a presence
a flaming mattress an important conversation
you barely go over in a jump you barely approach on all fours
the thorny borderland fenced with arrow signs that point
    to the closest post mortem hotels

Mariana Larrosa appears
drummer for her own dance
sprouted herb rope of her unique and inimitable swing

Tributo a John Coltraine: pelea 1 solo round con Jack Johnson

Para Pedro Damián Masson

Como sucede en estos apagones & arritmias de la vida
 1 aprende a apechugar a morder ácido
  a prender así sea a gritos el horno de 1 mismo

así sea partiéndose toda el ArcadeNoé contra el destiempo
 cabeceando por deporte delirio o descontrol
   por cada golpe e hinchazón
    por cada túnel raspadura atropellante precio

La sonrisa también la roba 1
 & la sangre en la que nada piel de nutria
  la obsesiva travesura

las danzas que endemonian & cesárean
 la necesaria aparición del aguacero-orgasmo
   & los mil & 1 ademanes furoanarcos
    con que en plena barriga del invierno embarazado
     1 quema sin diferencia de estaturas
      viejos amores & paraguas
& 1 come & caga / 1 se limpia & se vuelve a incinerar
       improvisando

astillándole música a la lava
 descascarándole besos de gorrión
  o fogatazos que 1 llama
   espejos quebrados / sal goteada de 1 mismo

costillas-corazón de vidrio clavículas alfilereadas por el susto
desprendimientos estallidos que todo terco tú
     correteas & los lazas

porque respiras ya / *así*
 como en lenguaje de trompeta
  como reciennacido & legendario jinete
   de estos búmerangs

Sonidos locos: sudores amplianervios

Tribute to John Coltraine: 1 Round Fight with Jack Johnson

For Pedro Damian Masson[60]

As happens in these blackouts & arrhythmias of life
  1 learns to take it on the chin to bite harshly
    to perhaps thus light with screams the very oven that 1 is

as would the ArkofNoah break apart against misfortune
  ramming for sport delirium or lack of control
    for every blow & head lump
      for every abrasive tunnel knockdown price

One also steals the smile
  & the blood in which an otter pelt swims
    the obsessive wickedness

the dances that bedevil & deliver by cesarean
  the necessary apparition of the cloudburst-orgasm
    & the thousand & 1 furoranarchist feints & moves
      with which in full belly of the pregnant winter
        1 burns regardless of stature
          old loves & umbrellas
& 1 eats & shits / 1 washes & goes back to incinerate
              improvising

shattering music to pieces at the lava
  flaying & peeling away sparrow kisses
    or great bonfires that 1 calls
      broken mirrors / salt leaking out of oneself

heart-ribs of glass clavicles pinned together by fright
explosive emissions that you so stubbornly
              chase after & lasso

because you now breathe / *thus*
  as though in a trumpet language
    like a recentborn & legendary jockey
      of these boomerangs

Crazy sounds: amplenerve sweatings

súbitos bailes que 1 abraza
   en apretado homenaje por los que ya bailaron
         —*nalgas al aire*
         1 volcán el pulso—
& dejaron huella / tatuajes que aún huelen /
  cicatrices viajeras: hemorragias que somos
    —babélicas ciudades bajo el hueso—
      terremotos que relinchan con pasión
        terremotos que dan ganas de ser tan vivo como ellos

& te hacen llorar / pero de risa
  como 1 árbol de charlots
    que te saluda levantando la patita

terremotos-terremotos-terremotos
 qué flor de terremotos
   terremotos preciosísimos

sudden dances that 1 embraces
  in tight homage for those who already danced
       —exposed buttocks
       heartbeat a volcano—
& they left a trail / tattoos that even now smell /
  traveling scars: the hemorrhages that we are
   —Babel-like cities beneath the bone—
    earthquakes that neigh & whinny with passion
    earthquakes that make one want to be as alive as they are

& they make you weep / but from laughter
  like a tree of Charlie Chaplins
   that greets you by lifting up its little foot

earthquakes-earthquakes-earthquakes
  such a bloom of earthquakes
   oh so precious earthquakes

Vas a morir como 1 ganglio de luz 1ue se ha vuelto loco vas a morir / entre silencios cojos

Para Sid Vicious & Elvis Costello

> Decir amor / muerte / hambre / sexo / ratas / de otro modo: para ser comprendido de otro modo /
>
> *José Revueltas / cárcel preventiva de la ciudad de México / octubre de 1969*

Elvis canta
  Elvis se quema
   se desgarra la garganta

Ha andado con suerte
el rock de la cárcel / no ha podido fundirlo

Sólo los espejismos moros se enamoran

La garganta se anuda
  & no llega a desanudarse

pero la luz que hay en mí
 se niega a extinguirse

No hay aerolito
al que no le pida STOP
no hay carretera
a la que no le arrebate 1 beso

Toco el día / en la calle
trepando postes de luz
ordeñando postes de luz
patinando vértebra a vértebra
esta ciudad de entrañas oscuras

la selva-apocalipsis de 1980 marchita mi paso

Alegría escupe zanjas
 Esperanza pare círculos
   Audacia se ahuma a sí misma
     Paradoja no sabe a qué otra circuncisión inciensar

You Will Die Like a Ganglion of Light that Has Gone Mad You Will Die / amid Crippled Silences

For Sid Vicious & Elvis Costello

> To say love / death / hunger / sex / rats / in another way: in order to be understood in another way /
>
> *José Revueltas[61] / preventive jail of the city of Mexico / October 1969*

Elvis sings
  Elvis burns up
   rips up his throat

He has been lucky
the jail house rock / hasn't been able to melt him

Only the mirroring Moorish mirages fall in love

My throat knots up
  & fails to unknot

but the light that is in me
  refuses to go out

There is no aerolith
that I would not beg to STOP
there is no highway
from which I would not steal a kiss

I touch the day / in the street
scaling lamp posts
milking lamp posts
skating through from vertebra to vertebra
this city of dark entrails

the jungle-apocalypse of 1980 withers my passing

Happiness spits out ditches
  Hope gives birth to circles
    Audacity fills itself with smoke
      Paradox does not know what other circumcision to burn incense to

hasta que *Saltomortal*
la despierta salpicándole cascadas
ríos de cul-de-sacs / callejones sin salida que son agua
saliva alfilereada de su propio mar de angustia
Vas a morir como 1 ganglio de luz
      que se ha vuelto loco
Vas a morir / entre silencios cojos

until the *Leap of Death*
awakens it spattering it with waterfalls
cul-de-sac rivers / blind alleys that are water
saliva fastened to its own sea of anguish
You will die like a ganglion of light
      that has gone mad
You will die / amid crippled silences

Despues del electroshock la bartolina

La medianoche sacude la memoria
como 1 loco sacude 1 geranio muerto

T.S. Eliot

En la estación *Mezcalina*
del Metro *Kimosari*

como 1 tlaconete
        que no nació para el andar rugoso
como 1 tlaconete
  al que le ha llovido demasiada sal

despierto vivo & excitado
 cantando *la balada de los huesos largos*
   que José Guadalupe Posada
   me ha enseñado en sueños

Tasajeándome —en forma de filetes—
  la mina-jardín de las delicias de las sienes
    excarvándome con clásicos dedos tepiteños
      la bolsa-morral marsupial de mis angustias

buscando hasta en la panza / plancha con púas / tenedor irritado de la muerte

1 esferita 1 gargajo de metal o hule
 con tal de seguir mondando las telitas-microondas
   el eco-escalofrío de esta vida tan alacrana & toque eléctrico
     tan pene sumergido / tan longdistance

Jalando con los dientes
  el fruto luz & espuma
    que cuelga como clítoris caliente
      de la minifalda-escalímetro del cielo
como dictado por la voz-carrera con vallas-saltotriple
 de 1 maromera energía extraterrestre

perro sin dueño
    clarasol sin lavadora

After Electroshock the Dungeon

> Midnight shakes the memory
> as a madman shakes a dead geranium.
>
> *T.S. Eliot*

In *Mezcalina* station
of the *Kimosari* Metro[62]

like a slug
    that was not born to go about shriveled up
like a slug
  upon which too much salt has been poured

awake alive & aroused
 singing the *ballad of the long bones*
   that José Guadalupe Posada[63]
   taught me in my dreams

Cutting out of me —in the shape of filets—
  the mine-garden of the delights of my temples
    digging out of me with classic Tepito fingers[64]
     the marsupial school bag of my anguish

searching even in my belly / for an iron with barbs / angry fork of death

a small sphere a wad of metal or rubberized phlegm
 continuing to peel off the little microwave fabrics
   the coldsweat echo of this life so scorpion & electric shock
   so submerged penis / so longdistance

Gobbling up with my teeth
 the fruit light & foam
  that hangs like a hot clitoris
   like the miniskirt scales of heaven
as dictated by the voice-run with triple jump hurdles
 of an acrobatic extraterrestrial energy

dog without owner
  chlorine without a washing machine

ladro & vuelo
  exploro & eyaculo
    pelo naranjas
      sombreo barrios
        circuncido lluvias
          encías de niñas / pubis de mujeres
              escalo & aleteo

 Como escapado de la indigestión-arenamovediza
  de 1 cuento de Allan Poe
   o 1 sueño-ardor tatuado por Fedor Dostoievski
recargado en nubes de pólvoramojada
 tembloroso como barro malcocido
 como venado cansado de bailar
   en las entrañas de las capillas funerarias
     donde Madame Tristeza-serpientecascabel
       les da de beber de su piquete
       a las hordas de huérfanos maltrechos
         que ha dejado el suicidiopasional
           de Doña Hiena & Don Coyote

& Mitos veo (con el calzón mojado & la chequera seca)
  cactus anémicos & 1 realidad que no florea
    mi misma voz me parece un gis eunuco / 1 brújula trabada
     1 collage tan sin branquias tan sin pulpa
       que el propio Max Ernst ya no sabe
         sobre qué puente de tricocéfalos kafkar
           bajo qué luna cucaracha tunelear
             con su tieso tenedor su bagazo sus cefaleas

Instantes hay
 en que hasta la ebria
   minotaura velocidad / de este universo-besonegro
   babea salpica se encabrita

garganta & recto
cerebelo & nalgas se confunden

El yo-chamán
 el yo-organillero-rutalibre
   hace / su / lucha / salva / sus /uñas

I bark & fly
  I explore & ejaculate
    I peel oranges
      I put barrios in darkness
        I circumcise the rains
          gums of little girls / genitals of women
                I climb & flap my arms

 Like an escapee from the dyspepsia-quicksand
  of an Allan Poe story
    or a dream-ardor tattooed by Fyodor Dostoyevsky
reloaded in clouds of wetteddust
 quivering like badly baked clay
  like a deer tired of dancing
    in the entrails of the funeral chapels
      where Madame Tristeza rattlesnake
        gives drink to the hordes of battered orphans
          from the points of her poisonous sting
            that has ceased the passionatesuicide
              of Doña Hyena & Don Coyote

& Myths I see (with wet underwear & dry check book)
  anemic cactus & a reality that does not bloom
    my own voice seems to me a chalk eunuch / a fastened compass
      a collage so without gills so without fleshy pulp
        that even Max Ernst himself still does not know
          over what bridge of tapeworms to Kafka[65]
            under what cockroach moon to tunnel
              with his rigid upright fork his bagasse his headaches

There are moments
 in which even the drunken
   minotaur speed / of this black-kiss universe
   slobbers spatters rears up in rage

throat & rectum
cerebellum & buttocks confounded

The I-shaman
 the I-freewheeling organ grinder
   makes / his / struggle / save for / his / fingernails

más allá de las murallas
   musicaliza zarandea
      el aura exploración desgañitada de sus albas

& está bien
 clarín-clarinetes de pájaros-estruendo
   No todos los días se celebra
     la comunión-cumpleaños de la pelvis

en las muelas cariadas del barranco
  el patín del diablo del furor
    / de puro gusto & puntada de tapiz extraño
(concubinato indesligable
   entre el hemisferio-zas & el hemisferio-cataplum)
se para de manos: se inventa nuevos éjeles

él mismo / su propia acupuntura-pararrayos
  él mismo / su muy particular & arropadito lago de aguamiel
en el que la estación *Mezcalina*
 del Metro *Kimosari*
 es apenas 1 dibujo / 1 crayonazo infantil de mis adentros

estos mis hornos que aún no escupen con fluidez sus propias desnudeces
  sandías-canción que tendrían en mi boca
    su inigualable cantante tragaldabas

sinfonolas que abanico desde *ya*
con este LP rayado que son desde mi no-nacimiento
                  mis costillas

Desconcertado pero firmes
 aguijoneado / pero en chinga
   pidiéndole a Lewis Carroll
    1 esquinita de su vuelo
      que me cuenta de los ojos-túnel cierto de su Alicia

& de 1 vez por todas me lo digo
 que no quede ni 1 fotocopia de mi sombra
   en los muros-telaraña de esta casa / de / la / risa

beyond the ramparts
   he sets to music he thrashes
      the halo shouted-out-loud exploration of his dawns

& it's all right
 clarion-clarinets of bird-bangs
   It is not every day that one celebrates
      the communion-birthday of the pelvis

in the decayed molars of the ravine
  the skate of the devil of the fury
    / of pure delight & stitching of a strange tapestry
(cohabiting inseparable
   between the ka-bang-hemisphere & the ka-boom-hemisphere)
one stands on one's hands: one invents new grids

he himself / his own lightning-rod-acupuncture
  he himself / his very private & cozy lake of honeywater
in which the *Mezcalina* station
 of the *Kimosari* Metro
 is barely a sketch / an infantile crayon scrawl of my inner self

these my hot places that do not yet fluidly spit their own nakedness
  song-watermelons that in my mouth would have
    their peerless gluttonous singer

jukeboxes that I fan from *now on*
with this scratched LP that are since my non-birth
                    my ribs

Disconcerted but unshakeable
 stung & goaded / but a fucking lot
   begging of Lewis Carroll
   a small bit of his flight
     that he tell me of the true tunnel-eyes of his Alice

& once & for all I tell myself
 that there remains not 1 photocopy of my shadow
   on the spiderweb walls of this house / of / laughter

No dejes 1 sola oportunidad

Para Patricia / Sierra-tortuga / antisiquiatra-mazateca / maestra-letra de corrido / amiga-cosquilla /
loca desigual & combinada / mujer-latidos de hongo / patafísica con plumas /
(la otra noche te soñé con plumas / patíbulo al alba)

No dejes 1 sola oportunidad
        con los dientes de fuera
Bienvenido sea a toda hora
                el beso de la diosa de la bugambilia imprevista
Llegue la madrugada
 con los ojos en arco
   los labios sin compás
    los bluejeans verdosísimos
Aparezca esa visión
  mordisqueando su armónica
    chillando a más no poder
      la fractura la confusión
                    de sus células
El paliacate que tú puedes girar en el aire
  el jarrito de café o marranilla
    que tú corres a frotar a otra boca
      que en plena embriaguez
va a abrazarte / chorrearte /
pasear muy muy alto
como sólo se puede poner a volar
a 1 túnel así de radiante
como sólo se puede emplumar
a 1 túnel con esas tus vísceras
            de ángel & cráter
Son apenas el tendón la articulación
        que la señora Soledad necesita
para empezar a poblar
            de colores & gritos sus calles
sus canales del parto / por el aserrín chamuscados
Sangren: crujan: relinchen
  sin calor sin acentos
    la boca-drenaje
      el interphone-taquicardia
        de estas horas violetas
Tú / deja de sobarle los huevos al tigre

Do Not Miss 1 Single Opportunity

For Patricia[66] / Sierra-turtle / Mazateca[67] anti-psychiatrist / master-letter of the corrido /
tickle-friend odd & mixed up madwoman / mushroom-throb woman / pataphysical with feathers /
(the other night I dreamt you had feathers / gallows at dawn)

Do not miss 1 single opportunity
       with your teeth showing
May the kiss of the goddess of the bougainvillea
         be welcome at every hour
Let the dawn arrive
 with its eyes in an arc
  boundless lips
   the most greenish of green bluejeans
May the vision appear
  nibbling at its mouth organ
   whimpering to the limit for
    the rupture the confusion
         of its cells
The scarf that you can twirl in the air
  the jug of coffee or cheap liquor
   that you rush to put to another mouth
    who in full drunkenness
will embrace you / squirt on you /
drifting by very very high
as only such a radiant tunnel
can be made to fly
as only a tunnel can be feathered
with those guts of yours
      of angel & crater
They are hardly the tendon and joint
    that lady Solitude needs
to begin to populate
     her streets with colors & shouts
her childbirth canals / scorched by the sawdust
They bleed: they raspingly grind: they shriek
 without heat without accentuation
  the sewer drain
   the tachycardia-intercom
    of these violet hours
You / stop fondling the tiger's balls

aplasta el huarache-garrapata
     de la Desolación & sus fábricas
Que estalle la Fiesta sin reversa sin frenos
       del orín-arcoíris
Sácate a bailar a la huraña rejega
     museógrafa araña
encerrada en los telares enyesados
    de tu página en blanco
Te imprima / no imprima su huella de semen
 el Carnaval de güiro & timbales
  los motines-ardor & Aventura
   que ya con su cuclilla fetal
    te han sublevado: enseñado a montar
     las bardas fibra-colmillo de vidrio
     de tu veladísima infancia
Ni por ganar la apuesta de los silencios peinados
 ni por mímica de merolico ranchero o teatro kabuki
  despellejes tu fuerza/ bajes tu volumen/ desconectes tus pilas

Tú eres todavía el reptil
 que viajó del mar a la tierra
  de la tierra a los aires
Tú eres todavía el lagarto que ríe
 el loro que habla
  el río de tucanes & garzas
   que esta tumba de esmog esperaba
Cochambre: asfixia
 parálisis: deshidratación
    / desencanto /
pueden ya emigrar
 con sus bozales quemados
 sus cantimploras vacías
Otro es el pito que hoy toca
con hojas de olmo
    raíces aéreas
las cuerdas vocales
 de estos machetes-lengüetazo de lobo
     picadura de abeja

navajas carnosas
 barbitas de axólotl

flatten the tick-infested sandal
        of Desolation & its factories
Let the Fiesta of the piss-rainbow without reverse
                without brakes explode
Take the reluctant hermit out to dance
            the reclusive spider
enclosed in the plastered weaves
        of your blank page
The Carnival of seaweed & drums
   primes you / it does not prime its trail of semen
     the ardor-mutinies & Adventure
        that now with their fetal curl
         have risen up against you: shown how to mount
            the walls of fiber-glass fangs
            of your darkest hidden childhood
Neither by winning the wager of the well-combed silences
   nor by mimicry of street ranchero or kabuki theater
      would you skin your strength / lower your volume / disconnect your batteries

You are still the reptile
   that traveled from sea to land
     from land to the skies
You are still the lizard that laughs
    the parrot that talks
      the river of toucans & herons
        that this grave of smog awaits
Filth: asphyxiation
    paralysis: dehydration
            / disenchantment /
can now migrate
   with their burnt muzzles
      their empty canteens
It is another whistle I now blow
with elm leaves
            air-borne roots
the vocal chords
   of these wolf lick machetes
                sting of a bee

fleshy blades
   wispy salamander whiskers

con las que se mueven los cactus
        las adrenalínicas luces / los desbocadísimos cláxons
                        de esta cuarteadura sin máscaras

            Viento-ungüento
            viento-brebaje
        para los bichos & yerbas
          piedras & sombras rodantes
            desiertos que arden
A la ½ de esta laguna
  temblorosa: muy breve
  conocida como el desfiladero sin brazos ni piernas
                        del orgasmo sediento

that cacti move around with
        the adrenaline lights / the blaring car horns
                        of this crack-up without masks
                Unguent-wind
                wind-concoction
            for the bugs & weeds
                rocks & rolling shadows
                    deserts that burn
To the ½ of this shallow lake
    quivering: very small
        known as the mountain pass without arms or legs
                        of the thirsty orgasm

Forjando 1 chaparrito flautín de Rhythm & Blues

Para el glucosaurio Gordon Ross

I

La punta más alta del cigarro hizo ¡Clic! & se apagó, velocidades de agua-láser trepaban las repentinas escaleras que la sola respiración del cerebelo —a lentos trancos— iba dando a luz. Los ojos eran buzos ya sin traje, nado, pulmones comprobables, agujeros con funciones de escafandra.

Desiertos brotacactus, baldíos sin cineramas, alcantarillas de asma que las pandillas utilizan como amplificadores-carne adentro de sus más urgentes maremotos musicales; sin tiempo, ganas, pulso necesario para marcar a palo-mojado en las paredes 1 mínimo homenaje a Dubuffet. A Dubuffet o a cualquier otro poro-mandril de nalgas có(s)micas de éste & otros vecindarios. La punta más alta del despegue hizo ¡Clic!, & ¡Zas! cantó.

II

Los callejones surgían, casi a voluntad de nuestros pasos. 1 paso levantaba 1 ceja, & a la hilera 2 de callejones le hacía ya sombra el silbido de la hilera 3. Toses más risas, comezones más tragedias desfilaban; maternidades, cementerios, manicomios, centros de recreo, uñas, pelos, grito & garraspera, que hacían tocable & hasta tibio el inexplicable desafío de querernos beber a pelosuelto el nervio en vida & el nervio ya sin cinto que dibujan a capricho el fórceps-laberinto que machuca a esta ciudad.

III

1 rato, salía el peine de la serenidad & me peinaba. Fuera de mis gestos, más allá de la cañería de mi sudor, pocos soles, menos fondos de mar ardían a mi alrededor o me besaban sin que se les deshidrataran las pilas o en mareante resplandor suicida repitieran: No sé / no sé / si penetrarte o reventarte. Como 1 dado en picada por los lavabos-débilsangre de tantos mataderos de este juego, yo mismo saltaba hacia atrás al escombrarme.

No sé / No sé / si penetrarme o reventarme. Cosmos cómico.

IV

La caricia (chorreante) de los nuevos hoteles solía redescubrirme los golpes, los vértigos (la aguacerosa presencia) de mi esquizofrenia feroz. Meduso-cantábile, alcohólico canal del parto, ocotemuevebosques de todos mis esfuerzos, nomadísima fogata / fulgurantísimo convoy / amuleto-imán hecho de venas / con el que más que abaniquearle las flamas al speech me la paso rebanándole 1 tajada, 1 tabique más al aullido concéntrico, al oxígeno hinchado de los besos; estos besos / estos besos; mientras forjo, con dulzura, 1 chaparrito flautín de rhythm & blues.

Hammering Out a Low Down Rhythm & Blues Piccolo

For Gordon Ross[68] the glucosaurus

I

The topmost point of the cigar went Click! & went out, water-laser speeds scaled the abrupt stairs that were given birth —in slow strides— by the sole breath of the cerebellum. Eyes were frogmen now without a suit, I swim, lungs demonstrable, holes with diving suit functions.

Cactus-studded deserts, wastelands without cineramas, asthma sewer lines that the gangs use as flesh-amplifiers within their most urgent musical tidal waves; without time, desire, the necessary impulse to mark a minimal homage to Dubuffet on the walls by means of a greased pole. To Dubuffet or any other mandrill-orifice of co(s)mic buttocks of this & other neighborhoods. The highest point of the take-off went Click! & Boom! It sang.

II

The alleys surged up, almost by the will of our footsteps. 1 step raised an eyebrow, & the 2nd swath of alleys was now overshadowed by the shrill whistling of the 3rd swath. Coughs more like laughter, annoying itches that were more like tragedies paraded by; maternities, cemeteries, madhouses, recreation centers, fingernails, hair, a scream & scratchy throat that make palpable & even tepid the inexplicable defiance of our wanting to drink with freeflowing hair the gristle in life & the now ungirded gristle that capriciously sketches the labyrinth-forceps that grinds up this city.

III

For a while, the hair comb of serenity appeared & combed me. Outside my gestures, beyond the plumbing of my sweat, a few suns, without sea depths burned around me or kissed me without drying up their batteries or in dizzying splendor repeatedly committed suicide: I don't know / I don't know / whether to penetrate you or piss you off. Like a dice pocked by the weakblood-washtubs of the many slaughterhouses in this game, I myself jumped back when I cleaned myself out.

I don't know / I don't know / whether to penetrate myself or piss myself off. Comic cosmos.

IV

The caress (squirting) of the new hotels tended to rediscover the blows for me, the vertigos (the cloudburst presence) of my ferocious schizophrenia. Cantabile-jellyfish, alcoholic birth canal, forestshakingbutthole of all my efforts, most nomad bonfire / most shine-stunning convoy / amulet-magnet made of veins / with him who more than fans the flames of speech I spend my time cutting him a slice, 1 more partition of the concentric howl, to the swollen oxygen of kisses; these kisses / these kisses; while I hammer out, in all sweetness, a lowdown rhythm & blues piccolo.

Arponeada la luna

Me duele la gangrena con las lluvias
el resplandor de existir : mi isla plena de ansias
el madrazo tatuado / el anclado sopor del altiplano
& tolteca crecí / aunque mareado
acosado por lentos cementerios
dentelladas reales : explosiones sin freno
que no son aún visión o embrión de mi astrolabio
Están meando las cuijas
está herido el umbral
mi infracueva sin párpados no resiste rendijas
Que la luz pinte puentes
que mis peces impulsen 1 motín / 1 trastorno
Que no haya ya niebla
que renazcan los ojos
Arponeada la luna remaremos a ratos
no le aunque el derrengue / el alacrán de la ira
Donde magia mana cae la gota erecta
zumba rocío en el andrajo
& si hay caminos opuestos / *los une el imán del alba*

The Moon Harpooned

Gangrene causes me pain with the rains
the resplendence of being : my island full of yearnings
the tattooed rebuke / the anchored down drowse of the high plains
& I grew up a Toltec[69] / even though dazedly
beset by slow cemeteries
real bitemarks : unbridled explosions
that are still neither vision nor embryo of my astrolabe
The little lizards are pissing
the threshold is wounded
my unblinking infra-cave is not crack-resistant
May the light paint bridges
may my fish start a mutiny / a disruption
May fog no longer be
may my eyes be reborn
The moon harpooned we will row at intervals
never mind the twisting course / the scorpion of wrath
Where magic flows the droplet falls standing on end
dew hums in the rags
& if there are opposing paths / *the magnet of the dawn unites them*

Saliva de San Juan Autista

Vueltas de carro de niños en la aurora
La madrugada del mundo pringosa / sanguinolenta /
                              se revuelca en su temazcal de júbilo
/ Manías que incendiarán tinieblas /
Si no es así
Asá serán las crematorias tuercas
Pinto mi librito de oro
Con las maromas sueltas de esta moronga tuerta
Rojo de coger / me asomo a cachar el aguacero azul
                       de tanta estrella ebria
Piso adrede lo que sé que soy
Aunque sea el sueño quien limpie de posibles precipicios
mi clavado tornasol
Amanezco con sardinas aún vivas
Excavando a fondo el azoro absurdo de mi calva humeante
Ni modo de elegir la muerte
Con la ternura en cueros & el oleaje denso
                de la frágil memoria descarnada
Me rasco pues con lo que tengo a mano
En mi breve Paraíso no crecen ni básculas ni encíclicas
Soy 1 delirium tremens que se inunda
Para que se bautice de bucito Dios

Saliva of Saint John the Autist

Comings & goings of toy cars at daybreak
The dawning of the world greasy / bloodied /
              shamefully sprawls in its bathhouse of jubilation
/ Manias that will burn up the darkness /
If it is not so
Thus will be the screwed up crematoria
I color my little book of gold
With the unfettered somersaults of this one-eyed blood sausage
Red from fucking / I go out to catch the blue downpour
                   of so many drunken stars
I willfully trample on what I know I am
Though it be the dream that would steer my bewildered sunflower
away from possible cliffs
I awake with still living sardines
Digging deep into the absurd panic of my steamy balding head
No way can I choose death
With tenderness stripped bare & the thick heaving waves
               of fragile bone-stark memory
So I scratch myself with what I have at hand
In my brief Paradise neither balance scales nor encyclicals thrive
I am a delirium tremens that is flooded
So that God may be christened a sea diver

Tierra colorada

I

Flagelo mi cuerpo con el foete indestructible del recuerdo
No he podido separarme de mi infancia
Sigo bebiendo en mis entrañas
absorbiendo las hemorragias de cicuta
Vale decir / sin pausas vivo
La ruta de la iguana a su misterio la he pisado garza a garza
incendiando los zarzales de mi cresta
La lengua del sol quema su hacha
Me atrevo a besarle la quijada
Este ovni-trompo aún me marca
Se me fuga la piel mordiendo su ancla

II

Estaba jugando a *soy yo mismo*
el eco de mi abuela & de mis sueños
el ángel que veía arder su sangre / como en legendario cine de gitanos
Estaba & aún estoy moviendo el barro
para poder tocar de 1 solo salto la hembra viva de esa cascada de albas

III

Froto de nuevo el fuego lúcido de trepar entre sombras la pus del tiempo
Sigo ordeñando cuanto me ocurre
Tras 1 guamúchil quiebro el cencerro
Ando mojado / camino al rastro
El Rey Lopitos está danzando 1 chilena en el Palmar
Trombas de historias
voces / peleas
saurios mulatos : ranas mestizas : hadas zumbando su majestad

Reddened Earth

I

I flagellate my body with the indestructible horsewhip of memory
I have not been able to separate myself from my childhood
I keep drinking within my guts
absorbing the hemlock hemorrhage
Needless to say / I live without pause
I have trod the iguana's route to its mystery heron by heron
burning the briar patches at the crown of my head
The tongue of the sun burns its hatchet
I venture to kiss it on the cheek
This spinning top UFO still shadows me
My skin slips away from me biting its anchor

II

I was playing at *I am myself*
the echo of my grandmother & my dreams
the angel that I saw burning his blood / like in the legendary Gypsy cinema
I was & am still moving the clay
so as to touch at one fell swoop the living female of that cascade of dawns

III

I again rub the lucid fire to scale the pus of time in the shadows
I go on milking whatever occurs to me
Behind a guamúchil[70] tree I break the cowbell
I walk on, soaked / I walk to the trail
King Lopitos[71] is dancing a Chilean girl in El Palmar
Windy storms of stories
voices / brawls
mulatto saurians : mestizo frogs : fairies buzzing their majesty

Sexus

Fogata de sudores encrespados
el agua lapizlázuli de este zeppelín nocturno
Cama casi carne / casi horno de enyerbados buriles giroscópicos
Aquí la hamaca de 1 óvulo en su trópico
la sangre lunar de tu hirviente submarino
la mermelada negra que revela al cuerpo en su exacto pantanódulo
/ virus siseante de pasional safari /
Aquí las fibras ocote-flor-toxina
las sales buitre-revólver-salsa roja
que dan / retiran
entrepiernan aliento & voz
tripulación más nave
memoria & hecatombes
Mares de arena glandular que nos inmundan
Aquí el sexo & su caparazón de gases
su hocico leve picapedreando espumas
los saltos de la ardilla por el túnel ebrio
la lengua de la loca luz labiodentando terso
Aquí el agua la yerba la caimana el perro negro
las cinturas de polvo / los monorrieles de pulpa
la esfinge como hongo en el ardor del obelisco
el aullido rotundo / la vibración de los sótanos
en 1 cráter que es hueso
trote / fragua / dentellada / risa loca / sensación de playa

Sexus

Bonfire of nervous sweat
the lapis lazuli water of this nocturnal zeppelin
Bed almost flesh / quasi oven of gyroscopic love-bewitched mason's chisels
Here the hammock of an ovum in its tropics
the lunar blood of your seething submarine
the black jam that reveals the body in its exact marshknob
/ hushed virus of passionate safari /
Here the butthole-flower-toxin fibers
the buzzard-revolver salsa roja salts
they give off / they withdraw
they crotch breath & voice
crew plus ship
memory & hecatombs
Seas of glandular sand that befoul us
Here sex & its carapace of gases
its weak slight snout stonecutting scum
the leaps of the squirrel through the inebriated tunnel
the tongue of the crazy light fluently labiodentaling
Here the water the herbs the she-caiman the black dog
the hips of dust / the monorails of pulp
the Sphynx like a mushroom in the ardor of the obelisk
the full emphatic howl / the vibration of the cellars
in a crater that is bone
trot / forge / toothed bite / insane laughter / sensation of seashore

Retrato dibujo de memoria en alguna estación del universo

A ésta la mataron cuando cabalgaba
quemando pestañas como crepúsculos en noches tan descoloridas
más allá de caminatas de caballo salvaje infinitas /
& se reía en la línea azul de las fronteras
cuando recorría vastos campos
donde pastaban búfalos & animales prehistóricos
grandes manadas de cohetes perdían su estela en el vacío /
ella salía de cavernas & alzaba los brazos saludando
intentando alcanzar las piernas de 1 muchacho
que sobrevolaba el territorio
A ésta la mataron cuando disparaba
          desde automóviles como piezas de museo
agitada desde el hueso
que brillaba como mar o farola rodeada de luciérnagas
quizás porque mostraba
cómodamente & sentidos afinados al interior de escondidos desfiladeros vegetales
(1 herida como roca
1 fulgurante lucidez de caimana
saboreando su pantano)
Maneras & sonrisas que le iban surgiendo como musgo
o escenas de coito veloz
a la manera de esos vientos-mito vientos-tótem
que ni en la compraventa de caricias se bajaban del caballo
Escenas sí situaciones
no previstas por el ojo-laberinto
                    el ojo-frente hinchada
que dice mirar & comprender
ése fuego-estampida respiración-alborotada
de larvas rodando cielo arriba

Portrait Drawn from Memory in Some Station of the Universe

This one they killed when she rode a horse
burning eyelashes like twilights in nights so discolored
far beyond any infinite wild horse jaunts /
& she laughed on the blue line of the borders
when she chased through vast fields
where buffaloes & prehistoric animals grazed
great herds of skyrockets lost their fiery wakes in the void /
she came out of caverns & raised her arms in greeting
attempting to reach the legs of a boy
who flew above the territory
This one they killed when she fired
            from automobiles like museum pieces
shaken to the bone
who shone like an ocean or street lamp surrounded by fireflies
perhaps because she displayed
with ease & sharpened senses the interior of hidden vegetal mountain passes
(a rock-like wound
a radiant lucidity of a caiman
savoring her swamp)
Manners & smiles that issued from her like moss
or scenes of quick coitus
after the manner of those myth-winds totem-winds
that even while buying & selling caresses would not dismount the horse
Scenes such situations
unforeseen by the labyrinth-eye
                the swollen eye-forehead
that says look & comprehend
that stampede-fire riotous-breath
of maggots rolling in the sky above

Alias El Socrates

El merolico calla
hipnotizado por la miseria de su público
La tromba se vislumbra irremediable
La sangre en la cabeza
escoge resortera & piedra
garfio & cascada
alucinación & salto
Es otra ya la calle que olfatea la catástrofe
El merolico piensa / haciendo gestos /
en 1 balsa promisoria que cruce las grietas de este tiempo condenado
La cloaca de Alcatraz no se abre hacia la Acrópolis
El incienso en la banqueta
roe de frente sus fronteras
El merolico vuela
Ya no ofrece pirámides ni excepciones a la regla
Flagela las nalgas esquizas de la vida
Monta toda clase de asfixias galápagas
Incinera la huida sofocada de la Esfinge
Como 1 meteoro más que se rompe el hocico
sin que su flor despierte ni 1 tantito a este mísero planeta

Alias Socrates

The street hawker falls quiet
hypnotized by the misery of his public
The inescapable cyclone looms into view
Blood in the head
chooses sling & stone
hook & cascade
hallucination & leap
The street is now another that smells the catastrophe
The street hawker thinks / making gestures
on a promissory raft that crosses the fissures of this condemned time
The cloaca of Alcatraz does not open toward the Acropolis
The incense on the curb
gnaws away at its borders
The street hawker flies off
He no longer offers pyramids or exceptions to the rule
He flagellates the schizoid buttocks of life
He rides every kind of tortoise asphyxiations
He incinerates the smothered escape of the Sphinx
Like 1 more meteor that breaks his snout
With his flower awakening not even a little to this miserable planet

Contrarretablo

Virgen eterna de la mescolanza
Jadeo genuino en vecindad horneada
Milagro siempre
Coral de luna
Cruel marejada
Pezón atroz
Nudo finísimo
Drenaje arisco
contra las rocas de la Tiznada
Mexicanita cuerva irizada
Mexicanita feta sin luz
Lágrima flaca
Madre volteada

Counter-Retablo

Eternal virgin of the helter-skelter
Genuine wheeze in oven-roasted vicinity
Miracle forever
Moon coral
Cruel sea swell
Atrocious nipple
Finest knot
Churlish sewer drain
against the rocks of the Blackened One
Mexicanita iridescent crow
Mexicanita fetus without light
Meager tear
Upside-down Mother

José Revueltas / el dia de su expulsion de la liga leninista espartaco

Esclavo inmigrante en el planeta Tierra
así me dicen sacándole el poto a la jeringa evidente de mis ojos
Aliento de taladro / patas de aguarrás
Yo amo como el Indio Bedoya en *Sierra Madre*
Port Clignancourt me achica el pito
Del *Hostal El Molinón* / no he arrancado ni aguas nimias
La estancia de mi ser : la sed de mi estandarte
Se llama *Locura total o me despido*
Miren qué contaminado de normales el bajovientre de esta estepa
Bugambilia marchita a la que se le escabulló el Deseo
Miren / absorbiendo
en la hora celestial del ojo
el peso de las hordas que celebran el furor
de 1 cuchillo que no olvido
La dialéctica tiene patas de cangrejo / Uyuyuyuy /
& al error de esta materia inanimada
que lo saje su chingada madre
porque yo ya me cansé
& de pilón 1 posdata:
Al ministerio de Disparates del País de Liliput
sólo ruego & deseo que se lo lave

José Revueltas[72] / the Day of His Expulsion from the Spartacus Leninist League

Immigrant slave on planet Earth
so they call me baring ass to the evident syringe of my eyes
Breath of auger / turpentine paws
I love like el Indio Bedoya[73] in *Sierra Madre*
Port Clignancourt shrinks my dick
I haven't drawn the least trivial waters / from *Hostel El Molinón*
The residing of my being : the thirst of my banner
It is called *Total madness or I take my leave*
See how contaminated with normality is the underbelly of this steppe
Bougainvillea withered by what Desire got away with
See / absorbing
in the celestial hour of the eye
the weight of the mobs that celebrate the furor
of a knife that I do not forget
The dialectic has the feet of a crab / Uyuyuyuy /
& upon the error of this inanimate material
may your fucking mother rip open
because I am weary now
& gratis a post script:
To the ministry of Foolery of the Land of Lilliput
I only plead & wish that they would wash it

Virgen & mártir del Rock & Roll

(In Memoriam John Lennon)

> Demasiada realidad puede ser 1 crucigrama
>
> *Theodore Roethke*

Su saliva aún gotea de los micrófonos calientes
Las tortillas de plástico (grabadas por millones)
mascan 1 & otra vez
el hígado inagotable
la clara necesidad de euforia
que bombeaba en sus canciones
Las huellas dactilares de su pulso
el teatro kabuki de sus gestos (ya verán en qué degenera esto muchachitos)
la Compañía Nacional de Subsistencias Populares de sus muecas vale madres
Los 1000 & 1 autorretratos de aliento giratorio
que la vida pública & los comités pro eterna adolescencia del show business
le arrancaron / a veces entre ¡bastas! ¡uffs! hastiantes hinchados zapatazos & alaridos
forzadas caminatas bajo el agua
sonámbulos paseos por los puentes colgantes del incienso
close-ups casi clínicos de su barba / de su calva
de su paso inclinadísimo como de joven viejo boxeador que va ablandándose
ya a punto del arpón & la piqueta / el cloroformo & el serrucho
Todos esos prismas & esos rostros
esos hilos & esos gramos
de su rebelde colchoneta mítica
son ahora charcos de su sombra ensangrentada
que los cuidadores del jardín (alias su historia)
no pueden limpiar ya
sin llevarse de paso & al galope
el perfume-resplandor de lo que 1 publicitado día
llegamos todos a saludar como al filete de sol de las orquídeas
fogata de baldío : pellejo de 1 sueño que ruega ser interpretado

Virgin & Martyr of Rock & Roll

(In Memoriam John Lennon)

> Too much reality can be a dazzle, a surfeit
>
> *Theodore Roethke*

His saliva still drips from the hot microphones
The plastic tortillas (recorded by the millions)
chew up again & again
the inexhaustible liver
the plain necessity of euphoria
that pumped into his songs
The fingerprints of his pulse
the Kabuki theater of his gestures (you will now see, little lads, into what this will
    degenerate)
the National Company of Popular Subsistence doesn't give a shit about his silly faces
The 1000 & 1 self-portraits of gyrating inspiration
that public life & the pro-eternal adolescence committees of show business
yanked out of him / at times amid fed up bombastic enoughs! ughs! kicks & shrieks
forced underwater marches
sleepwalking strolls over the suspension bridges of incense
almost clinical close-ups of his beard / of his bald spot
of his leaning gait like a young old boxer getting soft
now at spear & pike point / chloroform & bone saw
All those prisms & faces
those threads & those grams
of his mythic rebel sleeping mat
are now shallow pools of his blood-soaked shadow
that the caretakers of the garden (alias his history)
cannot clean any longer
without running off at a gallop
with the perfume splendor which 1 well-publicized day
we will greet like the sun streak of the orchids
wasteland bonfire : thin skin of a dream that begs to be interpreted

En busca del ave del paraíso

¿Se llamaba Ahmed / mula de carga
araña hablantina / chasis de tierra roja?

¿De qué manera lo tuteaban
los desfiladeros / los vientos color hormiga
que cada día eran su aureola / su sombrero / su chaleco de urticaria /
el plancton invisible —la goma caliente—
con la que él se entretenía & se sentía tan sensual
como 1 camello que se sumerge
en 1 mar aparecido de improviso?

Yo sé que lo vi 3 o 4 veces
(como esfinge arrodillada
por la ruta de las tumbas
de los 1^{eros} apóstoles cristianos)
1 viento de leones le besaba las mejillas
1 flotilla de ecos que surgían
como escapados del último muñón de Dios

In Search of the Bird of Paradise

Was he called Ahmed / pack mule
gibbering spider / red earth chassis?

In what way was he familiarly addressed
by the mountain passes / the ant-colored winds
that were his everyday aureola / his hat / his jacket of hives /
the invisible plankton —the hot gum—
with which he entertained himself & felt so sensual
like a camel that submerges itself
in an apparition of an improvised sea?

I know that I saw him 3 or 4 times
(like a kneeling sphynx
on the route to the graves
of the 1st Christian apostles)
a wind of lions would kiss his cheeks
a flotilla of echoes that surged
like escapees from the last vestige of God

¿A 10.000 millones de años luz?

¿A 10.000 millones de años luz?
¿Ahí fulge el vientre de Dios tatemado?
¿Sentado borracho en su invisible ataúd?
¿Jugando quemados con bombas e infantes?
/ Arrodillado bajo la inundación de sus párpados /
vislumbro su cerca & su junto
su falomatriz de orojade
su huizachal de zanates
su sombra que es luz
su neologismo encarnado
Me saluda sajándose
su cielo de sesos bullendo en hormigas
Es que Dios es cuitache
Es que Dios se las sabe
Él se coge a la semilla & al fruto
al zaguán / al tinaco / a la gata / a la hermana
En San Juan de Letrán lo conocen por Cuzco
en el bar Bataclán ha incendiado almorranas
El Carajo refulge hasta con sus nalgas esquizas
/ Es 1 manera de hablarle /
Está tan lejos que apesta
Con todo & su hachón de luciérnagas
& su manera de preparar el paté que sostiene la ilusión del océano

10,000 Million Light Years Away?

10,000 million light years away?
Is the belly of a sauced-up God shining there?
Drunk & seated in his invisible coffin?
Playing burn ball with bombs and infants?
/ On my knees under the inundation of his eyes /
I dimly sense his closeness & his nearness
his wombcock of jadegold
his huizache[74] grove of rooks
his shadow that is light
his coined word made flesh
He greets me cutting open
his heaven of brains boiling in ants
It's just that God is a pile of shit
It's just that God knows all the tricks
He fucks the seed & the fruit
the entryway / the water pot / the kitty / the sister
In San Juan de Letrán[75] he is known by Cuzco
in the Bataclán[76] nightclub he has set fire to hemorrhoids
The *Damn Prick* is refulgent up to his schizoid buttocks
/ It's a way of talking to him /
He is so far away he stinks
Along with everything & his big torch of fireflies
& his way of preparing the pâté that sustains the illusory dream of the ocean

Adolescensia bisiesta

Para Blaise Cendrars

Trabajaba entonces con cincel de kryptonita verde
        / fino & dañino /
Como pocos dientes de coyote
Como pocas ¡pocas! bolsas marsupiales
Acariciaba mi bragueta adelante & detrás de las ventanas
Novias chinas: golpe de suerte
& estribillos de esa índole
Escalinatas de Metro: mis sonrisas
Toboganes de espuma: mis miradas
Compases de 1000 puntas / cada paso
Martillos sin 1 clavo pero lluvias muy muy lluvias
                 mis bolsillos
Poesía crecía en belleza
Dormir era 1 despertar / en sus alvéolos
Manotearse el pelo: rehiletear 1 ojo
escupir caminos para los que chingan más que salvan
                 los zapatos
¡Dinero gratis! ¡autopistas gratis!
¡Aventones para Monte Albán!
Me enamoraba de llamas
Conversaba con ciempiés
Grabba en piel de yunque el chismorreo monosílabo
         que trompetean los semáforos
La ciudad me era tan labio / tan capullo / tan pezón
Jugaba con la doña a *la pared & los orines*
Hemoglobina no bajaba de ocurrente
Respirar me era tan Mark Twain / tan William Burroughs
      ...Burra cargada de...
Botella con mecha interna & hacia afuera
El desierto ¡por fin! derrotado por la voz
Mi pata de mambo: puro calcio
poniéndole semillas a la tierra
cascabeles a los botes
—disecando las baterías del adefesio—
Electrificando el espacio de los bailes
única & solamente con giros populares
Muy muy muy acompañado recalentado invadido de mí.

Leap Year Adolescence

For Blaise Cendrars

I worked back then with a green kryptonite chisel
                    / sharp & pernicious /
Like very few coyote teeth
Like very few (Very few!) marsupial pouches
I caressed the fly of my pants in front of & behind the windows
Chinese brides: stroke of luck
& refrains of that ilk
Metro stairways: my smiles
Foamy slides: my gazes
Beats of a thousand marks / each step
Hammers without 1 nail but rains, very very much rain
                              my pockets
Poetry grew in beauty
Sleeping was an awakening / in its lung cavities
Yanking one's hair: twirling 1 eye like a pinwheel
spitting roads for those who fuck around more than they take care
                              of their shoes
Money for free! Freeways for free!
Free rides to Monte Albán![77]
I fell in love with flames
I conversed with centipedes
I carved on the skin of an anvil the gossipy monosyllable
                    that the signal lights trumpet
For me the city was so labia / so cock head / so nipple
I played at *the wall & urine* with my lady
Hemoglobin was nothing short of whimsical
For me breathing was so Mark Twain / so William Burroughs
          …Donkey loaded with…
Bottle with a fuse on the inside & on the outside
The desert defeated by the voice (At last!)
My mambo hoof: pure calcium
attaching seeds to the earth
jingle bells to the tin cans
—taxidermizing the batteries of the outlandish figure—
Electrifying the space of the dances
with nothing but popular turns
Very very very accompanied overheated overwhelmed me.

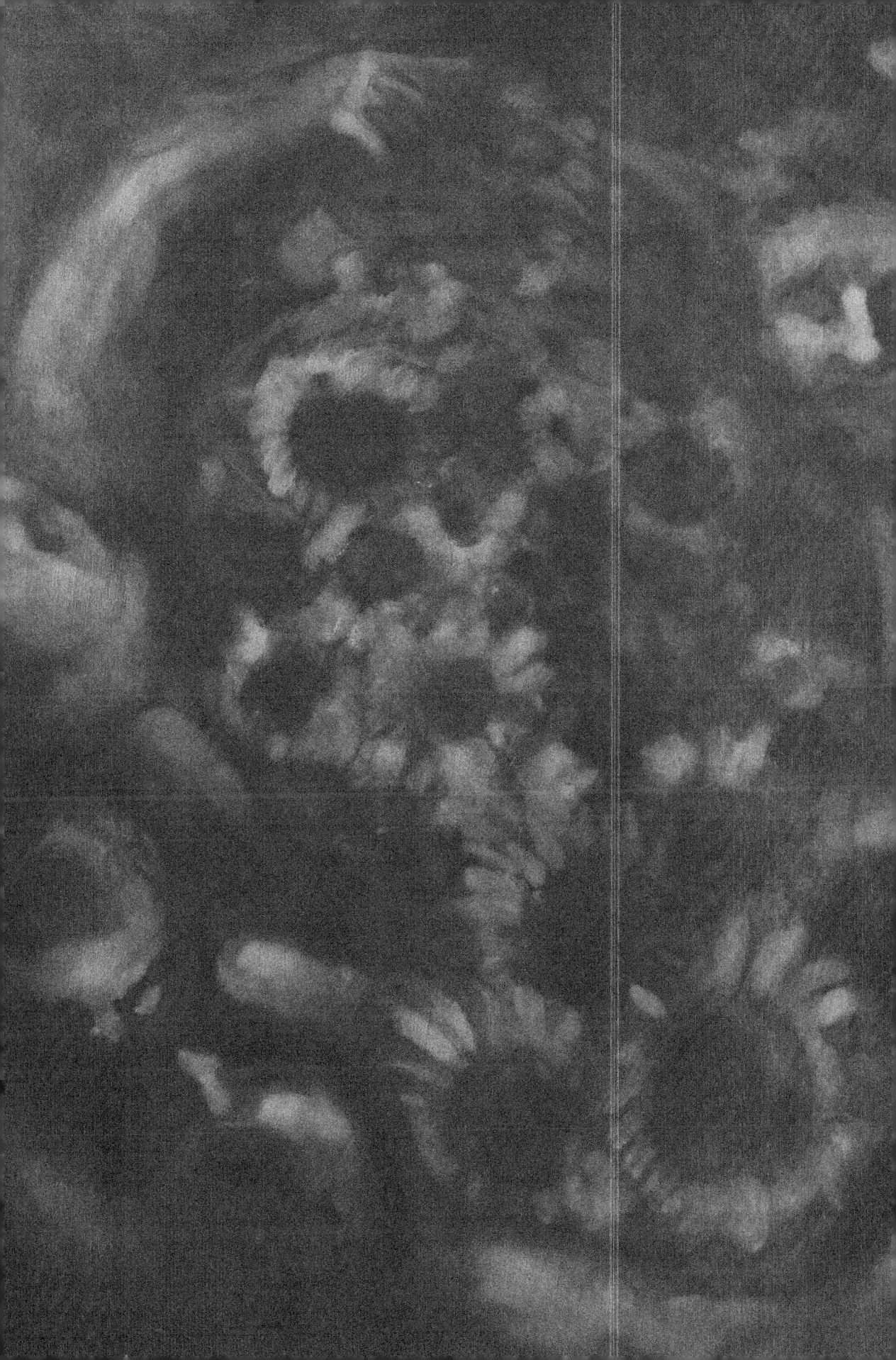

Las memorias de Peter Pan

Las portaviandas de mi infancia
/ el olor a gato ahogado /
los vastos cielos zopilotes
el buey solar sudando espejos
En las colas de los cines
la revelación / la lontananza
las carreras por el diesel
(los toreros de las julias)
los volados-arrecifes
Día tras día raspones muertos
/ envejecer & amachinarse /
conocer floreros-pozos
saporranas & gigantas
Por las calles del carajo
por comales / serpentinas / troles viejos / retortijones de canasta
El abuelo rocanrol aún fetito
la miseria / joven bruja
El asombro todo alas
por las tierras de encimita
bien arriba de las camas

The Memories of Peter Pan

The lunch boxes of my childhood
/ the odor of a drowned cat /
the vast buzzard heavens
the solar ox sweating mirrors
In line at movie houses
the revelation / the faraway distance
the diesel races
(the paddy wagon bullfighters)
the overhang coral reefs
Dead branches day after day
/ getting old & shacking up /
knowing flower-cesspools
toadfrogs & female giants
Through the dickhead streets
past braziers / winding ways / old trolleys / baskets of bellyaches
Rock & roll grandpa still a freak
misery / young witch
Astonishment totally on the wing
closely over the land
well above the beds

Hijos del Rey Lopitos

Nuestra aventura fue ésta:
—otro rayo en las bragas del caos—
Despertar / sumergirnos
Como ola la piel estrellada
En contextos no siempre reales
En los techos de Circe
—bugambilia fogosa—
el cristal de los cantos fue la forja
el afán / la escritura de días en océanos nublados
/ Cosmoalfiles /
Sex Raza
Elegimos el licor del insomnio al *speech* de la zarza
En playas de dunas
Bajo el coral que amaranta
& recordamos 1 prisma / 1 botón de mujer
en los hoteles del alba
Otra vez ruede & ruede
Experiencia flamígera / girasol de cascadas
El fulgor de los bosques
los *highways* sensoriales
Meteoritos de angustia
salpicando sus péndulos / tierra ardida / quema de llantas
Es 1 diapasón de la tribu
este gajo de luz en los dedos / la bacha / de la bacha
                                        más brava
En la ronda los cuates se transfiguraron carnales
No fue caspa del tiempo
Fue soñar otras danzas
El Watusi & el Chivo presumiendo de báquicos
El hotpant de la ninfa
/ le respondí a Vasconcelos /
Navegamos quemando
En la grieta: las plantas las enredaderas nerviosas
el nocturno acné que mandrilean las luciérnagas
El avispero del rol
En los barrios del perro chamán & la perra yerbera
& los hijos: hipnosis / hidalgos del puño del polvo
frotando el sol de su ruta
arenas abajo del viento / del diente / del sólido mar

Sons of King Lopitos[78]

Our adventure was this:
—another streak on the underpants of chaos—
Awakening / we swamp
The broken skin like a wave
In contexts not always real
On Circe's roofs
—fiery bougainvillea—
the crystal of the cantos was the forge
the eagerness / the writing of days on cloudy oceans
/ Cosmobishops /
Sex Raza
We elected the liquor of insomnia to the *speech* of the brambles
On beaches of dunes
Beneath the coral what amaranth
& we recall a prism / a woman's button
in the hotels of the dawn
Again it rolls & rolls
Flamboyant experience / sunflower of waterfalls
The splendorous flash of the forests
the sensory *highways*
Meteorites of anguish
peppering their pendulums / ardent land / burning of tires
It is the diapason of the tribe
this wedge of light on the fingers / bacchanal / of the fiercest
of bacchanals
In the revel the pals are transformed into brothers of the flesh
It was not the dander of time
It was to dream of other dances
The Watusi & the Goat putting on Bacchic airs
The hot pants of the nymph
/ I responded to Vasconcelos /
We navigate while burning
In the crevice: the plants the nervous tangling vines
the nocturnal acne that the fireflies monkey with
The hornet nest of the role
In the barrios of the shaman dog & the herbalist bitch
& sons: hypnosis / gentry of the fistful of dust
rubbing the sun from its path
sands under the wind / under the tooth / under the solid sea

Abluciones de escándalo
Los nudillos golpeando
La cantata ceñida al carril que trotamos
Cantarando & bailando
((la seda en la raya))
siemprevivas eternas
al sagrado & luminoso coito del bifronte amor
Sin importarnos chile piquín orégano estertores
                          ocotes o precio.

Outrageous ablutions
Knuckles rapping
The cantata pressed against the track we trot on
Chanting & dancing
((the silk on the stripe))
eternal sempervivums
to the sacred & luminous coitus of two-faced love
Chile piquín oregano death rattles Montezuma pine or price
                    of no importance to us

Desespejo

A la memoria de Beltrán Morales

Con musica de fondo de Javier Solís
1 Mural de alcohólicos el día
Explosión: la noche eterna
El viento encarnado en hueso florido de mujer
En vagancia de niños tras los sueños del flautista
Lo demás es muerte en vida
Convivencia de ratas & alacranes
/ *en tiempos & espacios diferentes* /
Pero atados al tufo que traza el arcoiris de 1 a otro horno
                              crematorio
Donde de seguro 2 locos reposan dándose 1 son
La bugambilia le rasca la ingle al polvo de la cruz
El sol es la multiplicación continua
El canto de la luz
El *tour de force* de lo creado
Que se mueve / sin embargo /
en el mundo —tordo gratis— como mariposa azul
Picasso se muerde la cola
—embarrado de follaje humano—
Silba el fantasma del globero
Suelta su hilo la semilla
La persigue ((entre navajas))
la certeza estratosférica del eco
La Belleza es nuestra Guernica espiritual
El retrato de Galatea empinándose en 1 pozo
/ culo fresco: *porno movie* de candor no natural /
Gordos & flacos ruedan por la herida abierta
El náufrago continúa en el agua / filmándose a sí mismo /
Tiempo de besar al destino
        ¡Como sea!
Está escrito en mi cuerpo encenizado
En la brama muda de otros cuerpos
que se abisman en el vientre aparente de sus yos
Todos somos Marías Sabinas conversando con los ángeles
Pero lo olvidamos / abrumados por la pena
                de no reconocernos
::Fracciones de segundo / lunas imantadas /
mordeduras de éter que masturban al sol::

Unmirror

In memory of Beltrán Morales[79]

           With background music by Javier Solís
A Mural of alcoholics the day
Explosion: the night eternal
The wind incarnate in flowering woman bone
In slothfulness of children behind the dreams of the flautist
The rest is death in life
Cohabitation of rats & scorpions
/ at different times & different spaces /
But tethered to the stench the rainbow traces from 1 oven to another
                                  crematorium
Where for sure 2 madmen repose letting loose a song
The bougainvillea scratches one's groin with the dust of the cross
The sun is continuous multiplication
The song of light
The *tour de force* of creation
That moves about / unimpeded /
in the world —a songbird given gratis— like a blue butterfly
Picasso bites his own tail
—coated with grime of human foliage—
The ghost of the balloon peddler whistles
The seed lets go its thread
Pursued ((with straight razors))
by the stratospheric certainty of the echo
Beauty is our spiritual Guernica
The portrait of Galatea rearing up in a hollow
/ fresh piece of ass: *porno movie* of an unnatural candor /
Laurels & Hardys[80] tumble through the open wound
The shipwrecked man lingers in the water / filming himself /
Time to kiss destiny
      Come what may!
It is written on my reduced-to-ashes body
In the mute bellow of other bodies
that plunge themselves in the manifest belly of their egos
We are all Marías Sabinas[81] conversing with the angels
But we forget it / weighed down by the grief
              of not recognizing ourselves
::Fractions of a second / magnetized moons /
bitten off pieces of ether that jack off the sun::

Tuve un sueño

En la reconstrucción de un catástrofe
En el siglo 23
El plasma de los muertos
Hablaba en un idioma único
Oxigenante hasta la lepra
Imagínate / "ciudadano lepra-oxígeno"
    (entre risas & voces de
    "el infrarealismo sigue actuando
    & / nada de grúas mecánicas /
    escaleras hechas de espíritu)
Frutas injertadas en verduras
Calenturas mechudísimas
Sin un solo rincón eunuco
El alba en su torpedo de tentáculos
En un par de parpadeos paría fuentes
A su frescura semejantes
La yerba buena la fumabas
Acompañado de tus mascotas de energía

I Had a Dream

In the reconstruction of a catastrophe
In the 23rd century
The plasma of the dead
Spoke in a one of a kind idiom
Filling up with oxygen until leprous
Just imagine / "oxygen-leper citizen"
    (amid laughter & outbursts of
     "infrarealism is still acting up"
    & / with no mechanical cranes /
    but ladders made of ghostly spirits)
Fruits grafted onto vegetables
The shabbiest unkempt fevers
Without a single eunuch retreat
The daybreak in its torpedo of tentacles
In 2 blinks of an eye gave birth to fountains
Similar to its own fresh newness
The good herb you smoked
Accompanied by your pet mascots of energy

Consejos de 1 discípulo de Marx a 1 fanático de Heidegger

A Roberto Bolaño & Kyra Galvan camaradas & poetas
Para Claudia Kerik & la suerte de haberla conocido

> También es hora
> de recordar que nada es bello
> ni siquiera en Poesía, que no es el caso
>
> *W. H. Auden*

El mundo se te da en fragmentos / en astillas:
de 1 rostro melancólico vislumbras 1 pincelada del Durero
de alguien feliz su mueca de payaso aficionado
de 1 árbol: el tembladero de pájaros sorbiéndole la nuca
de 1 verano en llamas atrapas pedazos de universo lamiéndose la cara
el momento en que 1 muchacha inenarrable
                se rasga su camisola oaxaqueña
exactamente junto a la medialuna de sudor de las axilas
& más allá de la cáscara está la pulpa / & como 1 extraño regalo del ojo
                                        la pestaña
Quizás ni el carbono 14 será capaz de reconstruir los hechos verdaderos
Ya no son los tiempos en que 1 pintor naturalista
rumiaba los excesos del almuerzo
entre movimientos de gimnasia sueca
& sin perder de vista los tonos rosazules de flores que no habría adivinado
ni en sus más dulces pesadillas

Somos actores de actos infinitos
        & no precisamente bajo la lengua azul
                de los reflectores cinematográficos
por ejemplo hoy / que ves cómo Antonioni se pasea
                con su camarita de rutina
observado por aquellos que prefieren enterrar la cabeza entre la yerba
a emborracharse de smog o qué sé yo / para que no aumenten
                                        los escándalos
que ya hacen intransitable la vía pública
por los que han nacido para ser besados largamente por el sol
& sus embajadores cotidianos
por los que hablan de coitos fabulosos / de hembras que no crees
                en esta edad geológica
de vibraciones que te harían tenaz propagandista del budismo zen
por los que se han salvado alguna vez

Advice from a Disciple of Marx to a Fanatic of Heidegger

To Roberto Bolaño & Kyra Galvan[82] comrades & poets
For Claudia Kerik[83] & my good fortune for having known her

> ...it's as well at times
> To be reminded that nothing is lovely,
> Not even in poetry, which is not the case.
>
> *W.H. Auden*

The world gives itself to you in fragments / in splinters:
in a melancholy face you dimly discern a stroke of Durer's brush
in someone happy the grimace of an amateur clown
in a tree: the shivering of birds sucking at the nape of its neck
in a summer in entrapped flames pieces of the universe licking its face
the moment in which an ineffable girl
                    rends her Oaxacan camisole
exactly at the halfmoon of sweat from her armpits
& beyond the peel is the pulp / & like a strange gift of the eye
                                        the lash
Perhaps not even Carbon 14 will be able to reconstruct the true facts
These are no longer the times in which a naturalist painter
would chew & rechew the excesses of lunch
between Swedish gymnastic movements
& without losing sight of the bluepink tones of flowers he could not have divined
not even in his sweetest nightmares

We are players of infinite acts
            & not precisely under the blue tongue
                    of the cinematography spotlights
today for example / you see how Antonioni strolls about
                    with his customary little camera
observed by those who prefer to bury their heads in the grass
to get drunk on smog or whatever / so as not to add to
                                        the scandals
that now clog the public thoroughfare
by those who were born to be kissed lingeringly by the sun
& its daily ambassadors
by those who speak of fabulous sexual couplings / of females you can't believe
                    in this geological era
of vibrations that could make you a stubborn propagandist of Zen Buddhism
by those who have been saved at some time

de los accidentes que la nota roja llama sustanciosos
& que de paso —por ahora— no se cuentan entre las flores del Absurdo

Así en el trapecio en el alambre de equilibrio
                              de este circo de 1000 pistas
1 abuelo platica la emoción que sintió al ver a Gagarin
                         revoloteando como mosca en el espacio
& lástima que la nave no se llamara Ícaro 1
que Rusia sea tan ferozmente antitroskista
                         & su voz entonces se disuelve / da de tumbos
                                   entre aplausos & abucheos

La Realidad & el Deseo se revuelcan / se destazan
se desparraman una sobre otra
como nunca lo harían en 1 poema de Cernuda
corre espuma por la boca de aquel que dice maravillas
& pareciera que vive en el interior de las nubes
                         & no en los baldíos de este barrio

El aire húmedo de abril / el viento lascivo del otoño /
         el granizo de julio & agosto
todos presentes aquí con sus huellas digitales

Alcohol
orines / qué no habrá servido de abono a esta yerba
cuántos jardineros sin el sueldo mínimo dejarán en esta trampa
              sus escasas proteínas

Por ahora tú te tiendes bocabajo a la sombra
              de las piernas largas & velludas de los parques
         donde se reúnen
el que sueña con revoluciones que se estacionan demasiado tiempo en el Caribe
el que quisiera arrancarles los ojos a los héroes de los posters
para mostrar al desnudo lo hueco de la farsa
la muchacha de ojos verdes gatunos & fílmicos
aunque a lo mejor acercándose resultan azules o quién sabe
el estudiante todo adrenalina & poros revoltosos
el que no cree en nadie / ni en la belleza kantiana
         de algunas admiradoras de Marcuse
& estalla gritando que estamos podridos por la furia /
deshidratados por tanto tomo de teoría

from accidents that the crime rag called substantial
& that by the way—for now—are not numbered among the flowers of the Absurd

Thus on the trapeze on the tightrope
                              of this thousand-ring circus
a grandfather chats about the emotion he felt on seeing Gagarin
                    circling around like a fly in space
& too bad the craft was not named Icarus 1
that Russia would be so ferociously anti-Trotskyite
                    & his voice then breaks up / he tumbles
                              between cheers & jeers

Reality & Desire are brought down / cut to pieces
one is scattered upon the other
as would never be done in a poem by Cernuda
foam flows from the mouth of the one who speaks marvels
& seems to live within the insides of the clouds
                              & not in the vacant lots of this barrio

The damp air of April / the lascivious wind of Autumn /
          the hail stones of July & August
all here present with their fingerprints

Alcohol
piss / that will not have done any good to this grass
how many gardeners without minimum wage would leave their scarce proteins
                    in this snare

For now you lay yourself facedown in the shadow
                    of the long & hairy legs of the parks
          where are gathered
he who dreams of revolutions that get stuck for far too long in the Caribbean
he who would like to pluck out the eyes of heroes in the posters
in order to show the naked man the hollowness of the farce
the girl with the catlike silver screen eyes
although close up they look blue or who knows what
the student all adrenaline & riotous pores
he who does not believe in anyone / not even in Kantian beauty
          of some of the female admirers of Marcuse
& he explodes shouting that we are putrefied by fury /
dehydrated by so many theoretical tomes

la putilla de ocasión que comparte el torrente de su soledad
                              con los desconocidos
dejando que la balanza de la oferta & la demanda la inclinen la gracia
              la simpatía las vibraciones repentinas
el Azar: ese otro antipoeta & vago insobornable
los que vienen aquí a llorar / hasta tallarse —como en madera—
                              1 rostro de mártir paranoico
después de destrozar —no precisamente de entusiasmo-
                              las butacas de los cines
el que escribe su testamento o su epitafio en 1 servilleta arrugada
& luego lanza besos al aire / —& todo el mundo supone
que celebra su cumpleaños o el divino himeneo de antenoche—
& todas las hipótesis resultan frágiles para explicar
por qué utilizó 1 pistola & no 1 bote de pintura
si parecía capaz de seducir hasta la calentura / el pulso
                              & la pupila del Giotto
el que siempre saluda con un *Yo estoy desesperado*
                              ¿& usted?
los que se aman rabiosamente como perros callejeros
              –en las verdes & en las maduras–
& 1 los llama enamorados floridos
& son 1 afrodisíaco no sólo para la sensibilidad de Marc Chagall
los que conocen en persona a la muerte
a la hora en que el suicidio se vuelve 1 obsesión
unas ganas despeinadas de morder & ser mordido
de poner 1 hasta aquí a tanto castillo de arena
                              que parece inderrumbable
de inventarse por segundos 1 Poder
que las revolvedoras de cemento cotidianas te desbaratan
              como si fueras 1 papel de estraza

& entonces comprendes al que quisiera sepultar
                    bajo toneladas de plantas
                    edificios / tierra negra
el menor latido / la taquicardia de su historia íntima
te contagia el nerviosismo la intranquilidad
              de los que hacen como que respiran
como que poseen 1 cierto dejo de plantas carnívoras
& se pasan horas esperando a la compañera Ternura
              esa call-girl que raras veces llega
los que vienen escapando de los gases lacrimógenos

the bargain basement skank who shares the torrent of her solitude
                        with complete strangers
letting the balance of supply & demand be tipped by grace
                sympathy sudden vibrations
Chance: that other antipoet & incorruptible loafer
those who come here to weep / until they carve —as in wood—
                the face of a paranoiac martyr
after destroying —not exactly out of enthusiasm—
                                the plush seats of movie theaters
he who writes his testament or his epitaph on a crumpled napkin
& then throws kisses to the wind / —& the whole world assumes
that he is celebrating his birthday or the divine epithelium of the night before—
& all the hypotheses turn out to be too flimsy to explain
why he used a pistol & not a paint can
if he were able to seduce even the feverish desire / the pulse
                                & the eye of Giotto
he who always greets you with *I am desperate*

                                        & you?

those who love each other rabidly like stray dogs
                —in sweetness & in bitterness—
& one calls them flowery innamorati
& they are an aphrodisiac not just to the sensibility of Marc Chagall
those who know death in person
at the hour in which suicide becomes an obsession
some disheveled cravings to bite & be bitten
to be fed up to here with such a sand castle
                                that seems indestructible
to dream up within seconds a Power
so that ordinary cement mixers might shred you
        as though you were a piece of butcher paper

& then you understand he who would entomb
                        beneath tons of plants
                                buildings / black earth
the slightest beat / the tachycardia of his intimate history
you are infected by the nervousness the disquiet of those who
        do things the same way they breathe
the same way they possess a certain aftertaste of carnivorous plants
& hours pass waiting for Tenderness the play mate
        that call-girl who on rare occasions comes
those who show up escaping from tear gas

& las macanas de las grandes avenidas
de las grandes & las pequeñas manchas que ya no tienen remedio
con aroma de pino o la caricia de 1 kleenex
los que ignoran quiénes son / *ni lo quieren saber*
cuando el clima tiene peor fama cada día
los eternos enfermos de amnesia que se chupan el dedo de alegría
porque aquí & no en Miami está el Paraíso Terrenal
los que juran declarar esto territorio libre isla independiente
que no degenere en chatarra ruina supermarket

En el instante en que 1 canción de moda
   enreda su ritmo
a la peculiar batucada de la lluvia
& se instaura 1 orden fatalmente momentáneo
para que sigan dominando la escena
   el cabello en desorden /
     los enormes ojos húmedos
& como surgida del claroscuro mismo de la noche
aparece 1 niña con los puños embarrados contra los muslos
repitiendo 1 / 2 / 3 veces:
Yo no soy 1 objeto sexual / no lo soy robots /
    estoy viva / como 1 bosque de eucaliptos
aquí donde la norma es ser implacablemente amables
     los unos con los otros
  & este es el mal menor

El parque tiembla / mis pasos interiores me llevan
por las calles de 1 puerto de mar verde
    que los nativos llaman *Mezcalina*
  1 sensación hasta ahora desconocida
como saber a ciencia cierta a qué sabe el ADN
   después de hacer el amor

Si esto no es Arte me corto las cuerdas vocales
mi testículo más tierno / dejo de decir tonterías
   si esto no es Arte

La rama de 1 árbol se dobla bajo el peso de 1 gorrión
o mejor dicho 1 gorrión termina por hacer trizas 1 rama ya quebrada

  Aún estamos con vida

& the night sticks of the grand avenues
of the big & little stains that now cannot be fixed
with the scent of pine or the gentle wipe of a Kleenex
those who are unaware of who they are / *& do not want to know*
when the weather is more disreputable every day
the perpetually ill from amnesia who suck their finger happily
because here & not in Miami is the Earthly Paradise
those who vow to declare this territory free independent island
that shall not degenerate into a junk-ruin supermarket

In the instant that a hit song
        coils its rhythm
around the peculiar samba drummings of the rain
& an order is installed fated to be momentary
that they may continue to dominate the scene
        so that the shock of hair of disorder /
                & the enormous watery eyes
& as though issuing forth from the very chiaroscuro of the night
there appears a little girl with muddy fists against her thighs
repeating 1, 2, 3 times:
I am not a sexual object, I am not, you robots,
                I am alive / like a forest of eucalyptus
here where the norm is for all to be implacably friendly
                with each other
        & this is the lesser evil

The park trembles / my steps within myself take me
through the streets of a port by a green sea
                that the natives call *Mezcalina*[84]
        a heretofore unknown sensation
like knowing with scientific certainty what DNA tastes like
        after making love

If this is not Art I will cut my vocal chords
my most tender testicle / I will stop saying foolish things
                if this is not Art

The branch of the tree will bend under the weight of a sparrow
or better said a sparrow will end up breaking to pieces an already broken branch

        We are still with life

de alguna manera hay que llamar a las islas de cristales
que con lujo de violencia patean las zonas más blandas de tus ojos
la realidad parece de mica de miniatura a escala
pero también tus párpados tu percepción & su camisa de fuerza
                              la Materia & la Energía /
& el ánimo para meter tu lengua entre su lengua

Éste es 1 día insólito
vibrante cotidiano anónimo
terrícola a más no poder como solemos decir los días de fiesta
            o durante los cateos cada vez más frecuentes de las casas
el miedo te ilumina el estómago & te lo quema

NO HAY ANGUSTIA AHISTÓRICA
AQUÍ VIVIR ES CONTENER EL ALIENTO
& DESNUDARSE

—Consejos de 1 discípulo de Marx a 1 fanático de Heidegger—

Poesía : aún estamos con vida
                  & tú prendes con tus fósforos mi cigarro barato
                  & me miras como a 1 simple cabello despeinado
temblando de frío en el peine de la noche

                        Aún estamos con vida

1 mariposa ojoverde & alas amarillas
            se ha prendido en la solapa azul de mi chamarra
-mi cuerpo de mezclilla
            se siente seductor radar humano imán de polen
adquiere por momentos la convicción de 1 galaxia en pequeñito
            cantando puras locuritas entre ohs de asombro-
¡Pucha qué luna!
exclama el millonario en soledad
                        & mísero en empleo
al que apenas ayer lo despidieron porque no le emocionaban
los cortocircuitos de la cafetera burocrática

¡Qué luna!

it is necessary in some way to call to the isles of crystals
that with the luxury of violence kick the softest zones of your eyes
reality seems like mica miniature in scale
but so do your eyelids your perception & your strait jacket
                              Matter & Energy /
& the spirited will to entwine your tongue with its tongue

This is an unprecedented day
vibrant ordinary anonymous
earthling in the extreme as we tend to say on festive days
                    or during the ever more frequent house raids
fear lights up your stomach & burns it

THERE IS NO AHISTORICAL ANGUISH
HERE TO LIVE IS TO HOLD ONE'S BREATH
& GET NAKED

—Advice from a disciple of Marx to a fanatic of Heidegger—

Poetry: we still have life
                    & you light my cheap cigar with your matches
                         & you look at me as you would a simple unkempt head of hair
trembling with cold in the comb of the night

                         We still have life

a green-eyed & yellow-winged butterfly
                    has alit on the lapel of my jacket
—my blue denim body
                    feels like a radar seducer human magnet of pollen
it acquires at times the conviction of a galaxy in miniature
                    singing sheer minor madness between Ohs of amazement—
Shit & onions what a moon!
exclaims the millionaire in solitude
                              & a wretch at work
who just yesterday was fired because he was not excited
by the short circuitings of the bureaucratic coffee maker

What a moon!

como uña cortada
            como 1 gajo de esperma
                suspendido
sobre el lomo crispado de la noche

cuando se escucha
1 crujir de nueces aplastadas —crac—
el zumbido el lloriqueo de 1 ambulancia
                que otra vez no llega a tiempo
el rumor de las lagartijas con manchas de leopardo
trepando traviesísimas por la enredadera en busca de alimento
los últimos ruidos de 1 picnic
                donde la Desolación ha hecho de las suyas
& ha acabado voceando la proximidad del viento
                que todo mancha & roe

Sin embargo 1 aún camina por aquí como gorrión feliz
como Chaplin el día en que besó por primera vez a Mary Pickford
alguien pasea con 1 radio de transistores
                                que parece su segunda oreja
Galileo descubre la ley del péndulo observando
                        el columpiar dulzón de estos amantes
violentamente unidos & medioconsumidos por la niebla
creyendo los muy necios que el Amor a dentelladas
                        terminará por brillar en technicolor

& esto en el mismo m² / a la misma hora
en que el polo norte & el polo sur
la tesis & la antítesis del mundo
            se conocen
como 1 aerolito incandescente & 1 ovni en problemas
e inexplicablemente se saludan:
Yo soy el que se ha grabado en la espalda de la chamarra de mezclilla
la frase: El núcleo de mi sistema solar es la Aventura
me llamo así pero me gusta que me digan *Protoplasma Kid*
Tú eres el que se muerde las uñas mientras hojeas la sección de crímenes
con los dedos confundidos en lo tieso de la hoja de periódico
            pero
¿son las noticias /
    los que las reportan /
        los que las leen como 1 droga necesaria?

like a clipped nail
        like an arc of sperm
        suspended
over the black withers of the night

when one listens
a crunch of crushed nuts —crack—
the whirring the whining of an ambulance
        that once again does not arrive on time
the rustle of little lizards with leopard spots
daringly scaling the creeper vine in search of food
the last noises of a picnic
        where Desolation has been up to its tricks
& has finished singing out the proximity of wind
        that sullies & gnaws away all

Nevertheless one still walks through here like a happy sparrow
like Chaplin the day he kissed Mary Pickford for the first time
someone strolls by with a transistor radio
        that looks like his second ear
Galileo discovers the law of the pendulum observing
        the very sweet swinging of these lovers
violently united & half-consumed by the fog
the headstrong pair believing that Love nibble by nibble
        will end up shining in Technicolor

& this in the same square meter / at the same hour
in which the North Pole & the South Pole
the Thesis & Antithesis of the world
        are known
as an incandescent aerolith & a UFO in trouble
& they inexplicably greet each other:
I am he who imprinted on the shoulder of the blue denim jacket
the phrase: The nucleus of the solar system is Adventure
That's my name but l like to be called the *Protoplasm Kid*
You are the one who bites his nails while leafing through the crime section
with your fingers puzzled by the stiff pages of the newspaper
        but
are they the news /
    those who report it /
        those who read it like a necessary drug?

¿Quiénes Sherlock Holmes son los asesinos?
Dadas las circunstancias desconfías hasta de tus propios ojos
forcejeos corretizas pleitos de qué calibres
        se esconden bajo las ropas más rasposas
los miedosos se trepan a los árboles
los más ágiles prefieren andar señalando con el dedo
el momento exacto en que la atmósfera se enrarece hasta decir basta
& comienzan a derrumbarse los aviones como en 1 secuencia de cine mudo
en la que los brazos de los moribundos se mueven como aspas
sin explicarse el por qué de ese horizonte ensalivado por el fuego

Aunque el cielo —aparentemente— se vea sobrio & despejado
como enemigo irreconciliable de las Artes Plásticas
& casi nadie repare en el loquito que besa lame muerde su reloj sin manecillas
mientras pregunta ¿¿¿*Se estará enfriando la tierra*
        no nos estaremos saliendo de la órbita???
seguro de que en 1 caso así hasta Jerry Lewis lloraría sinceramente

En cualquier momento acontece 1 poema
        por ejemplo
ese aleteo de moscas afónicas
        sobre 1 envoltorio que nadie acierta a descifrar
cuánto tiene de basura & cuánto de milagro
        por ejemplo esas colegialas con los libros apretados contra el pecho
que hacen que gire la cabeza de 1 hombre de canas & lentes traqueteados
mientras el viento —lúbrico— juguetea bajo sus falditas
        Por ejemplo
el gordo & el flaco que duermen la siesta
        soñando las mismas travesuras
donde el pastel quiere servir de maquillaje
& 2 pies están necios en entrar donde cabe 1 sólo pie
        por ejemplo
el que apenas ayer —disfrazado de mujer— se fugó de la clínica siquiátrica
& no se cansa de pararse de manos & corre como canguro loco
        preguntándose por el sentido de la vida
por 1 mertiolate que le borre sus moretones interiores
        los rasguños de la insulina & los electroshoks
mientras canta en forma de balada aquel verso de Guido Cavalcanti
        Ya que no espero nunca más volver
        por ejemplo
ese muchacho pelirrojo que se remoja los pies en el agua de la fuente

Who Sherlock Holmes are the murderers?
Given the circumstances you doubt even your own eyes
struggles chases quarrels of such dimensions
                    are hidden under the coarsest clothes
the fearful climb the trees
the more agile prefer to go about pointing out with their finger
the exact moment in which the atmosphere thins until they say enough
& the planes begin to plummet & crash as in a silent movie sequence
in which the arms of the dying move like windmill sails
without explaining the why of that horizon salivated by fire

Even though the sky —apparently— looks sober & cloudless
like an irreconcilable enemy of the Plastic Arts
& almost no one notices the loony who kisses licks bites his handless watch
while he asks *Is the earth becoming cold*
            won't we fall out of orbit???
certain that in such a case even Jerry Lewis would weep sincerely

At any given moment a poem will occur
        for example
that wing beating of soundless flies
            over a plastic bag about which no one can figure
how much of garbage & the miraculous it contains
            for example those schoolgirls with their books clenched to their chests
who make a man with graying hair & rickety glasses turn his head
while the wind —lewdly— frolics under their little skirts
            For example
Laurel & Hardy who take a nap
        dreaming of the same pranks
in which cake is used as make up
& 2 feet stubbornly try to go where only 1 foot will fit
            for example
he who just yesterday —disguised as a woman— escaped from a psychiatric clinic
& who never tires of standing on his hands & who runs like a crazed kangaroo
                    pondering the meaning of life
about some merthiolate that would eliminate the inner bruises
                    the scratched tracks of insulin & electroshocks
while he sings in the style of a ballad that verse of Guido Cavalcanti
            Now that I have no hope of ever returning again[85]
        for example
that red-haired boy who dips his feet in the water of the fountain

& se siente Huckleberry Finn viajando en 1 balsa de troncos
/ en pleno Missisipi /
o 1 barbudo clochard llenándose los pulmones de tabaco turco
a la orilla del Sena
viendo su nombre escrito sobre el agua: *Lord xyz*
mientras la realidad navega como 1 barco de vapor ruidoso & agitado
porque sabe que la vida puede hacerle morir & renacer
a cada instante
–en 1 tiempo & 1 espacio
donde no cuentan Euclides ni su geometría de balbuceos–
& lo inmediato lo peliagudo de los días que corren
se ve representado por cualquier fulano que grita ¡Auxilio!
& marca el 06 de su conciencia
para enterarse qué marca de vida o desperdicio le corresponde besar
escupir o mirar horrorizado
cualquier fulano que grita o lo intenta & no puede
mientras el asombro se dibuja (como con cera quemada)
en su rostro rígido de obrero jubilado
que parece & de qué manera
1 bomba de tiempo

En momentos / en el chisguete en que 1 segundo vomita & palidece
todo es trágico / hasta la alegría / la que quieras /
Esquilo & Harold Lloyd jugando ajedrez con corcholatas de cerveza
pero sin saber cómo calcios hacer crecer su ocio creativo
a la altura de 1 terremoto que sea de verdad borrón & cuenta nueva
Cuando el Caos se ve robusto hasta lo bestia
(facha de toro & voz de marica)
cuando sobra decir que se está económicamente cagado
(Tú / Yo / Nosotros)
para no hablar de la neurosis & la anemia *made at home*

& de qué sirve entonces de qué sirve
el huracán la tómbola de cosas
que te desnudan & te invaden como amibas
de qué sirve si tú no entiendes por qué sobrepoblación
por qué abortos
1 mujer encinta te sonríe /
si no capizcas si es de desesperación o de contento
que se palmotea la barriga como la Virgen del Parto de Piero de la Francesca
si sólo alcanzas a tartamudear a dilatar los ojos

& feels like Huckleberry Finn traveling on a raft of logs
                              / in the middle of the Mississippi /
or a bearded clochard filling his lungs with Turkish tobacco
                              on the banks of the Seine
seeing his name written on the water: *Lord XYZ*
while reality sails like a noisy agitated steam boat
because he knows that life can make him die & be reborn
                              at every instant
—in a time & a space
        in which neither Euclid nor his babbling geometry count—
& the immediacy the dodginess of the days that fly by
        is represented by any so-&-so who yells "Help!"
                        & dials the 911 of his consciousness
in order to find out what brand of life or waste it falls to him to kiss
                        spit on or look at horrified
any so-&-so who yells or tries to & cannot
        while astonishment is drawn (as with melted wax)
on his stiff retired laborer's face
        that looks —& how!— like
                        a time bomb

In just moments / in the spurt when 1 second vomits & pales
all is tragic / even happiness / whatever suits you /
Aeschylus & Harold Lloyd playing chess with beer bottle caps
but without knowing how the fuck to increase their creative leisure
        to the level of an earthquake which would be truly clearing the board &
    starting over
when Chaos appears robust even animalistic
                                (a bull's face & a sissy's voice)
when it is needless to say that we're economically in the shit
                (You / Me / Us)
not to mention neurosis & *home-made* anemia

& of what use is it then of what use is it
            the hurricane the raffle drum of things
                    that strip you naked & invade you like amoebas
what use is it if you don't understand why overpopulation
        why abortions
                    A pregnant woman smiles at you /
if you don't capeesh whether it's out of desperation or contentment
that she palms her belly like the Virgin of Childbirth by Piero de la Francesca

cuando entra en función la mano eficaz del carterista
/ ese discípulo de Shiva el de los 7 brazos : Dios de la masturbación
& el asalto de factura fina /
si sólo alcanzas a tragar saliva & a hacer gestos
cuando ese personaje de Ionesco —quizás traumado por la cantante calva—
a las primeras de cambio te pregunta: ¿está usted sexual política
vitalmente satisfecho?

& de qué sirve que el rocío que exprime la gardenia
en la madrugada neblinosa
te lo conozcas tan a pulso como la palma de tu mano
como el pubis —sabroso— de la muchacha
que es el relieve de tu mapa
& la brújula que mantiene en pie tu territorio

de qué sirve si hay vidas que son 1 automóvil sin motor
tocando el cláxon desesperadamente
sin poder partir

la de aquél que se cura la cruda sabatina mojándose los ojos
en los bordes de las fuentes
la de la señora de la high con su peinado de crema chantilly & charamusca
& su vocecita inaguantable cuando dice *Yo fumo de los míos*
toda esa raza de momios de gestos sagrados
que se sienten ofendidos
por el roce cada vez más frecuente con la plebe
entre el hollín & el sol gruñón de las ciudades
& la vida de aquel vagabundo (el que el vox-populi dice que no falta)
el que tiene la lucidez hecha pedazos / sin que su bicicleta
haya perseguido luz alguna en la Sierra Tarahumara
como su homónimo Antonin Artaud

la de aquel que da demasiadas vueltas para besar 1 flor
encender 1 cigarrillo
decirle a la amada: vamos a 1 hotel / reventémosle a la luna
esa cara de patata blanca
la del burócrata despistado /que se equivoca & más de 2 veces
el que va a tener la misma cara de telenovela
—compadecida de sí misma—
la próxima que pase por aquí

if you only manage to stammer on dilating your eyes
when the skillful hand of the pickpocket goes into action
            / that disciple of Shiva he of the 7 arms : God of masturbation
& the finely crafted assault /
if you only manage to swallow saliva & make faces
when that Ionesco character —perhaps traumatized by the bald soprano—
at the first opportunity asks you: are you sexual political
                              vitally satisfied?

& of what use is the dew expressed by the gardenia
            in the hazy dawn
you would know it like the palm of your hand
as well as the mons pubis —delicious— of a girl
that is your relief map
                  & compass that keep track of your territory

of what use is it if there are lives that are cars without motors
            desperately honking the horns
            unable to depart

that life of him who cures his Saturday hangover by wetting his eyes
                  beside fountains
the life of the high society lady with her Chantilly cream & sugar twist hairdo
& her insufferable little voice when she says *I smoke my own*
        that entire breed of right-wing stiffs with sanctimonious faces
              who feel offended
by their more & more frequent brushes with the rabble
        amidst the soot & the ill-humored sunlight of the cities
& the life of that vagabond (there is no lack of him according to popular opinion)
he whose lucidity has been shattered / without his bicycle
        having pursued any light in the Sierra Tarahumara
as did his like-named Antonin Artaud

the life of him who goes through too many gyrations to kiss a flower
                                    to light a cigarette
to say to his love: let's go to a hotel / let's bust up that potato-white
        face of the moon
the life of the absent-minded bureaucrat / who is mistaken & more than twice
he who will have the same melodramatic face
                  —that look of self-commiseration—
the next time he passes by

la de la ex reina de la primavera en tiempos de Hiroshima
        & ahora abuela neurótica de trillizos mongoloides
la del adolescente sin dinero & dispuesto a todo
        & con caderas que le hubieran estrangulado el pulso a Oscar Wilde

la del cursi que dice que 1 parque
        es como el hígado florido de 1 ciudad
mientras bailotea sobre la punta de los pies
        alrededor de 1 mujer que no le ha dicho ni su nombre
la de tantos & tantos que se han bañado 5 / 6 veces
        en las aguas negras del fracaso
& no por gusto (dicen ellos)
no como quien se come —entre sonrisas— 1 tartaleta de merengue
        de ninguna manera así
& eso es lo que siempre dices (Tú / Yo / Nosotros)
mientras te abrochas lentamente el impermeable
        -el cuerpo & tus defensas sicológicas-
& sales a dar 1 vuelta —que será más de 1-
        bajo la lluvia
            dentro & fuera
        bajo la lluvia
& todo porque necesitas te urge soltarte a llorar sin disimulo
sin que nada ni nadie te interrumpa
ni aquellas chavalas en hotpants
        brillando con sus muslos de bronce
& abrazadas a los rubios postes de luz

& no eres el único que proclama ser el único pasajero
        de su submarino esquizofrénico
mientras caminas (como ido) con el cigarrillo apagado en la boca
& la lluvia escurriéndote de manera grotesca
        desde el ojo a la barbilla

Desde luego que no eres el único
frente al que el paraguas oxidado de la vida
        no quiere desplegar sus alas
no eres el único al que el mundo le parece
—en 1 momento pesimista-
1 ghetto sin puentes ni caminos

& a veces también tú cojeas & te oscureces

the life of the ex-queen of spring in the times of Hiroshima
       & now the neurotic grandmother of mongoloid triplets
the life of the teenager penniless & up for anything
       & with hips that would have stifled the heart of Oscar Wilde

the life of the cheesy snob who says that a park
       is like the florid liver of a city
while he minces about on tip toe
       around a woman who hasn't even told him her name
the life of so many who have bathed 5 / 6 times
       in the black waters of failure
& not because they like it (they say)
not like someone who eats—while grinning—a meringue tartlet
       by no means whatsoever
& that thing you always say (You / Me / Us)
while you slowly buckle up your raincoat
       —your body & your psychological defenses—
& you go out to take a walk —which will be more than a walk—
       in the rain
          inside & out
       in the rain
& all because you have to you are compelled to weep openly
without anything or anyone interrupting you
not even those gals in hotpants
       flashing their bronze thighs
& with arms wrapped around the blond lamp posts

& you are not the only one who claims to be the only passenger
       on his schizophrenic submarine
while you walk (as if out of your mind) with a spent cigarette in your mouth
& the rain grotesquely trickling down
       from your eye to the tip of your chin

Of course you are not the only one
for whom the rusted umbrella of life
       does not want to unfold its wings
you are not the only one to whom the world seems
—in a pessimistic moment—
a ghetto with no bridges or roads

& at times you too limp around & become gloomy

te rascas la nariz & la costra del recuerdo
        la Existencia toma el cuerpo de 1 policía
que te pasea su macana último modelo a todo lo largo de la cara
& tú todavía preguntas: ¿Qué onda mi lobo feroz?
        ¿Qué tal de salud la represión?
mientras tiemblan las matas de mariguana
sembradas como zanahorias en el subsuelo de tu mente
& tu corazón es 1 vecindad populosa
        con las coladeras & el techo derrumbándose
        por el puro miedo
                por el puro miedo

Con todo sobreviven el oxígeno & el giro acompasado de los astros
Septiembre nos guiña 1 ojo
& es mejor si cada quien se abraza a su cintura más querida
1 perro cocker color miel continúa sumido en el séptimo sueño
mientras 1 mosca canalla utiliza de sofacama su nariz
basurillas cáscaras papeles
vuelan enredadas en las valencianas del viento
que hoy puede trozar 1 flor
                golpearla luego sobre el suelo
pero mañana /
        adiós bióxido de carbono /
apoplejía perra suerte Adiós
Explícale a tu amigo ocasional
        que hasta 1 erección fallida
forma parte del proceso

esto / & el bermellón chingón de los crepúsculos
& el vuelo de los tordos que ennegrece por 1 momento el aire
& la flama de vida que alborota el vello de tu pecho
en las épocas decisivas
& con toda la pinta de volverse Historia Épica

Explícale eso a tu amigo ocasional
        esclarécetelo a ti mismo

que la vida siga siendo tu taller de poesía
& ojalá electrifiques la energía de tu tormenta interior
junto a la muchacha con agilidad de velero
que has elegido como la compañera de tus próximos brincos

you scratch your nose & the scab of memory
          Existence assumes the body of a policeman
who lays his latest-model nightstick along the entire length of your face
& still you ask: What's up my ferocious wolf?
          How's the repression going?
while the marihuana bushes tremble
sown like carrots in the subsoil of your mind
& your heart is a crowded neighborhood
          with its rain gutters & roofs tumbling down
          out of sheer fright
                    out of sheer fright

Nonetheless oxygen & the regular spin of the stars survive
September winks its eye at us
& it is better that everyone hugs the waist that he most loves
a honey-colored cocker spaniel continues lost in the seventh dream
while a despicable fly uses its nose as sofa bed
bits of garbage rinds papers
fly around tangling in the trouser cuffs of the wind
that today can pick apart a flower
                    then strike it to the ground
but tomorrow /
          farewell carbon dioxide /
apoplexy bitch luck Good-bye
Explain this to your sometime friend
          that even a failed erection
is part of the process

this / & the badass vermillion of the twilights
& the flight of the thrushes that momentarily blacken the air
& the flame of life that ruffles the down on your chest
in the decisive epochs
& with all the colors of becoming Epic History

Explain this to your sometime friend
   make it very clear to yourself

that life is still your poetry workshop
& here's hoping you electrify the energy of your inner storm
together with the girl who has the agility of a sail boat
whom you have chosen as a companion for your coming caprices

que el amor o la demencia que más se le aproxime
te habite / te aligere los talones
te lustre el brillo de los ojos
Ojalá / ojalá

Los fragmentos las astillas de hace rato
se hacen en manos como las de Houdini
1 grito tan sólido & real
como 1 seno o 1 manzana
o 1 deseo que hace de todo cuerpo 1 prisma transparente

Lo aparentemente estático & fugaz
resulta ser 1 pieza de valor en el tablero:
detrás de 1 simple fotógrafo ambulante
habitó alguna vez 1 tal Ernesto Che Guevara
& no parecía capaz del menor esfuerzo sudoroso
para no hacer mención de hazañas éticas

Lo aparentemente estático & fugaz
resulta 1 pieza de valor en el tablero:
el aliento & el ardor que te acompañan
cuando recorres avenidas kilométricas
recordando los versos la piel de Safo
bañada por la luna
cuando te pasas la mano por la cara
en el momento en que eres 1 arcoíris
rasguñado por el sol & la garúa de las 4 de la tarde
cuando escribes sobre el torso desnudo de los árboles
los artefactos poéticos de este fin de siglo:

Te amo el resto
You turn me on
Tú me enciendes
¿Cómo puede ser esto
tan hermoso?

—ardiendo de fe
& entre oleadas de placer—

Cuando ves en esto el instinto de la lucha por la vida
que ponía eufórica a Rosa Luxemburgo

may the love or dementia that strikes closest to home
                    dwell in you / lighten the load on your heels
burnish the shine of your eyes
          Let us hope / let us hope

The fragments the splinters of a while ago
          become in hands like Houdini's
a scream as solid & real
as a breast or an apple
or a desire that makes all bodies a transparent prism

That which is apparently ecstatic & fleeting
turns out to be a valuable item on the board:
behind a simple itinerant photographer
                    there once lived a certain Ernesto Che Guevara
& he didn't seem capable of the least strenuous effort
not to mention ethical deeds

That which is apparently ecstatic & fleeting
          turns out to be a valuable item on the board:
the breath & ardor that accompany you
          when you travel miles of avenues
recalling the verses the skin of Sappho
bathed by the moon
when you run your hand over your face
in the instant that you are a rainbow
clawed at by the sun & the dreary rain of 4 in the afternoon
when you write on the naked torso of the trees
the poetic artifacts of this turn of the century

                    I love every part of you
                        You turn me on
                    You light my fire
                    How can something be
                        so beautiful?

—burning with faith
                    & between heaving waves of pleasure—

When you see in this the instinct of fighting for one's life
          that made Rosa Luxemburg euphoric

la práctica en vivo del teorema favorito del hereje Wilhelm Reich:
1 cuerpo se alfabetiza junto a otro cuerpo
        & así se funda la Universidad de la Ternura

cuando aprendes a decir No
        con toda la energía de 1 karateca cintanegra
o a decir Sí / con la certeza
        de que pronto las estrellas tendrán 1 color
que hasta pasado 1 buen rato entenderemos

Lo aparentemente estático & fugaz
        amenaza con incendiar & a besos
la hora en que las grandes insurrecciones políticas parecen enterradas
(así dicen los economistas burgueses desde sus introspecciones antiaéreas)

Pero 1 aún ve a la vida
        digna de 1 tatuaje hecho a mano
aunque por ahora se pose para 1 fotógrafo invisible
        que puede ser el mismo clima que arde

Aunque por ahora sólo parezca
        que la Belleza se radicaliza emotivamente
como playeras multicolores que dicen: *Kiss me*
                desde la zona más erógena de sus torsos

como 2 mocosos (se rumora son jipis o anarcoides)
        que prometen encontrarse
        a tal hora / en tal puesta de sol
en el Puerto Ray Bradbury de los canales de Marte
/ A como dé lugar
                exactamente allí /
Bajo 1 cielo por el que Van Gogh daría las gracias en 6 idiomas /

¿& qué blancura añadiréis a esta blancura
        qué aliento / qué ardor?

the living application of the favorite theorem of the heretic Wilhelm Reich:
a body becomes literate together with another body
        & so was founded the University of Tenderness

when you learn to say No
        with all the energy of a black belt in karate
or to say Yes / with the certainty
        that soon the stars will have 1 color
which we will understand after a good amount of time

That which is apparently ecstatic & fleeting
        threatens to burn & with kisses
the hour in which the great political insurrections seem buried
(so say the bourgeois economists from their anti-aircraft introspections)

But 1 still sees life
        worthy of a hand-fashioned tattoo
even though for now it poses for an invisible photographer
        who could be the same burning climate

Even though for now it would only seem
        that Beauty is movingly radicalized
like multicolored t-shirts that say: *Kiss me*
        from the most erogenous zone of their torsos

like 2 snotty kids (it's rumored they are hippies or anarchists)
        who promise to meet up
        at such & such an hour / at such & such a sunset
in Port Ray Bradbury of the canals of Mars
/ No matter what
            right there /
Beneath the sky for which Van Gogh would give thanks in 6 languages /

& what whiteness would you all add to this whiteness
        what breath / what ardor?

Endnotes

1— Carte d'Identité: This autobiographical prose poem was addended to *Aullido de cisne* (*Swan's Howl, 1996*), the sole collection published prior to Mario Santiago Papasquiaro's death.

2— …infrarealist from the very start: Mario Santiago was, along with Roberto Bolaño, one of the principal founders of the "infrarrealista" literary movement. *See also Note 11 and Note 12.*

3— Jorge Negrete (1911-1953): A popular Mexican singer and film star.

4— Sacred Flock of Guadalajara: The reference here is to the soccer team Club Deportivo Guadalajara, popularly known as "los chivas" (the nanny goats).

5— *Dialectics of Nature*: *Dialektik der Natur* by Friedrich Engels.

6— goblin: Santiago uses the word "chaneque," which was a small sprite-like being, an elemental force and guardian of nature, according to pre-Columbian Mexican lore.

7— José Revueltas (1914-1976): A writer and an activist within the Mexican Communist Party whom Mario Santiago admired and considered a literary and political progenitor. Revueltas was jailed after being accused of being the brains behind the student protest movement that culminated in the Tlatelolco massacre in Mexico City in 1968.

8— …giant salamander: *ajolote* (*axolotl*) in the original.

9— Oliverio Girondo (1891-1967): Argentine ultraist poet whose last work, *En la masmédula (In the Ultra-marrow)* was seen as an avant-garde effort in which he employed Joycean portmanteau words and coinages.

10— …a barrio brass band: Mario Santiago uses the slang term "chile frito," literally a fried chile, referring to funky itinerant bands of amateurish musicians that prowl the poor streets of Mexico City.

11— Roberto Bolaño (1953-2003): Chilean poet and novelist and author of the acclaimed novel *Los detectives salvajes (The Savage Detectives)*. When he was 15, his family relocated to Mexico City where he attended secondary school and began writing poetry in earnest. In 1974, he met Mario Santiago, and the two became fast friends and co-conspirators, disrupting poetry readings and lectures given by the literary elite and making Octavio Paz a particular target. Bolaño used Santiago as the model for the character Ulises Lima in *The Savage Detectives*.

12— …founder of a movement: A reference to *infrarrealismo* (Infrarealism) and its adherents, it was a literary movement founded in Mexico City by Mario Santiago and Roberto Bolaño. Consisting of a loosely-knit group of some 20 poets, its members included such notable writers as Rubén Medina, Ramón Méndez Estrada, and José Rosas Ribeyro. While the movement wasn't never completely defined, Bolaño once referred to it as "a sort of Mexican Dadaism."

13— Guadalumpen: Here Mario Santiago uses "Guadalupe," the name of the iconic virgin of Mexico who was based on the Aztec goddess Tonantzin (*See Note 18*), and melds it with the German word *lumpen*, from the Marxist term *lumpenproletariat*, workers of the lowest order.

14— Mañanitas: Traditional Mexican romantic morning serenades, usually sung to women.

15— …Her woven palm mat is my mat of palm (*Su petate es mi petate*): The petate has long served as a bed and resting place for the humblest of Mexicans, many of whom are born on a petate and die on a petate.

16— Juan Diego (1474-1548): First indigenous Roman Catholic saint of Latin America (canonized in 2002). He was said to have witnessed four apparitions of Our Lady of Guadalupe near Mexico City on Tepeyac Hill in 1531.

17— Butterfly Dog: Mario Santiago seems to use this as an alternate name for Juan Diego. However, Juan Diego's pre-baptismal Nahuatl name was Cuauhtlatoatzin, meaning "Little Talking Eagle."

18— Tonantzin: A Nahuatl honorific roughly translated as "Our Lady" and as such, can be applied to a number of goddesses. Traditionally, the goddess who appeared to Juan Diego has been identified as the Goddess of the Earth or the Goddess of Maize.

19— Huichol: An indigenous Mexican people inhabiting the Western Sierra Madre. The consumption of hallucinogenic peyote is central to their religious rituals and customs.

20— Lophophora Williamsii: Peyote, a small, bulbous cactus without thorns, whose flesh is ingested for its psychoactive properties.

21— …In the gateway of the clouds: "Gateway" is one possible translation for the Spanish word (of Arabic origin) "zaguán". A zaguán, in Moorish architecture, is a covered entry-way into the central courtyard of a house, a patio around which the rooms of the house proper are arranged. The word has come to signify a doorway, a vestibule or foyer. The phrase makes reference to a stage of a physical and spiritual journey made yearly by the Huichol. Each year the Huichol make pilgrimage to a high desert called "Wirikuta" where they gather and eat peyote in order to communicate with their ancestors and gods. To reach Wirikuta, the Huichol must climb past two plateaus: "Cloud Gate" and "Where the Clouds Open."

22— Wirikuta: High desert location where the Huichol people make pilgrimage to gather, eat peyote and communicate with their ancestors and gods. *See also Note 21.*

23— *Álvaro Carrillo*: This is most likely Álvaro Carrillo Alarcón (1921-1969), Mexican song writer who wrote the classic bolero *Sabor a Mí*.

24— Richard Belfer (1954-): A journalist, literary editor and poet who appears to have been of significant interest to both Mario Santiago and Bolaño.

25— Mara Larrosa: A member of the Infrarealists; Mara and her sister Vera were fictionalized as "the Font sisters" (María and Angélica) in Bolaño's novel *The Savage Detectives*.

26— For Esther Cameo & Mauri Pilatowski: At the time of publication, these persons could not be identified with any certainty.

27— Richard Brautigan: Mario Santiago contributed translations of the work of Brautigan to the Mexican review *Plural* (October 1976, Volume 61).

28— Carnal: A difficult word to translate succinctly. Used almost exclusively among Mexicans and Chicanos, it is a word of recognition of brotherhood and racial identity; similar to the African Americanism "Blood," its use conveys a call and appeal to the very flesh of another.

29— …Saint Elizabeth keeps on wounding hides & souls: Most likely a reference to St. Elizabeth's Hospital in Washington DC, the mental institution where Ezra Pound was confined for 12 years in lieu of incarceration for treason.

30— Chilpancingo: Capital of the Mexican state of Guerrero.

31— Jehovah's Witness: In the original, "tejón" means "badger," a slang term for proselytizing Jehovah's Witnesses.

32— Lecumberri: A notorious prison in Mexico City that held numerous political prisoners from 1900 to 1976. Beginning in 1980, it housed the national archives of Mexico.

33— Carnal: *See Note 28.*

34— Leopoldo María: Leopoldo María Panero (1948-2014). The greatest Spanish poet of the latter half of the 20th century, who spent most of his life in insane asylums.

35— Rebeca López (1966 2011): Rebeca López García was Mario Santiago's wife and mother of his two children. She, more than anyone else in his life, provided him with love, security, and support. As his widow, she compiled and published, along with Mario Raúl Guzmán, an extensive collection his poetry, *Jeta de Santo.*

36— For El J.C.: Refers to the great Argentine novelist Julio Cortázar (1914-1984).

37— la Maga: meaning "Magician" or "Sorceress," it refers to a character in Julio Cortázar's novel *Hopscotch* (*Rayuela*). La Maga is a mysterious, intriguing woman for whom the protagonist—a figure based on Cortázar himself—searches throughout Paris. La Maga is said by some to be based on Alejandra Pizarnik. *See Note 39.*

38— Tlaxcalteca: A predominantly Nahuatl-speaking nation in Mexico at the time of the conquest. They were allies of the Spaniards, and, as a result, governed their lands autonomously after the conquest and were granted various privileges.

39— Alejandra Pizarnik (1936-1972): Argentine poet and translator of Antonin Artaud, Henri Michaux, and Aimé Césaire. She claimed that she was the character "la Maga" in Cortázar's *Hopscotch.*

40— Alebrijes: Common items found in curio shops that carry Mexican crafts and folk art and are brightly painted wooden figures of real or imagined animals and people.

41— molcajete: A mortar and pestle made of volcanic rock and used in Mexico for grinding spices and grain.

42— atole: From the Nahuatl "atolli," it is a porridge typically made with toasted corn meal mixed with brown sugar and cinnamon. Rice or oatmeal is sometimes substituted for the corn meal.

43— huazontle: Hairy amaranth, from the Nahuatl "huanutli" (amaranth) and "tzontli" (hair). Its botanical name is *chenopodium nutalliae*. The plant is used as a vegetable and herb in Mexican cooking.

44— chinampas: A system of agriculture, comprised of cultivated plots of earth that were built up on shallow lake beds. Held together by wicker and reeds and rooted by stakes to the lake bed, they and the crops growing on them could be dislodged and floated via canals to Tenochtitlan, the capital of the Aztecs.

45— Germán Valdés: Also known as "Tin-Tan," he was a Mexican film star, singer, dancer, and wild antic comic actor. He was raised in Ciudad Juárez along the U.S. / Mexico border, where he absorbed a great deal of American popular culture. He was instrumental in introducing the culture, language, and style of the Pachuco to Mexico. In many of his films, he sported a zoot suit, broad-brimmed hats, and long, ostentatious pocket watch chains.

46— Tongolele: Stage name of Yolanda Yvonne Montes Farrington (1932-). Born in the United States, she studied Tahitian dance forms, performed in Mexican theaters and cabarets and appeared in numerous films, including several with Germán Valdés, also known as Tin-Tan. *See also Note 45.*

47— Tin-Tan: *See Note 45.*

48— Enthcogenic: From the Greek *entheogen*, "generating God within." Enthcogenic refers to any psychoactive substance that induces a spiritual experience and is aimed at spiritual development. Entheogens are used by curanderos to heal people but also by malevolent sorcerers to steal their energy.

49— …Rubén is his name & he is my dear carnal: The reference here is to Rubén Medina, Santiago's friend and poet and founder of the infrarealist movement. He has published an infrarealist anthology, *Perros habitados por las voces del desierto* (*Dogs Haunted by the Voices of the Desert*). Medina is currently a professor of literature at the University of Wisconson, Madison.

50— Infraín: A name given to the poet/journalist Efraín Huerta by Mario Santiago and other infrarealists. (The name is a melding of "infra" and "Efraín.") Mario Santiago admired Huerta's political stances and his approach to poetry and considered him and José Revueltas (*See Note 7.*) his spiritual fathers. A Stalinist and advocate for the downtrodden, Huerta developed and practiced a sort of "anti-poetry," characterized by a realistic, colloquial style.

51— Órale: Mexican slang interjection signifying approval and/or encouragement similar to "Right on!" It also serves as an enthusiastic greeting.

52— Pablo de Rokha (1895-1968): Avant-garde poet, considered to be, along with Pablo Neruda and Gabriel Mistral, one of the great modern-day poets of Chile. An anti-fascist political activist, he was a member of the Chilean Communist Party.

53— Bilboquet: "Baleros" in Spanish, a toy having a cup or spike at the top of the stick with a ball and string.

54— …5 mountains: Apparent reference to the 5 Great Mountains of Chinese lore to which pilgrims made excursions to make offerings.

55— Tlamatinimes: From Nahuatl "tlamatini," meaning "a wise man," one who operates in life in shamanic ways.

56— Reality tlacoyos: A tlacoyo is a thick, oval-shaped tortilla stuffed with a variety meats, cheese, beans, and chiles. Mario Santiago seems to be making a reference here to the "reality sandwiches" that Allen Ginsberg writes about in his poem "On Burroughs' Work": "… A naked lunch is natural to us, / we eat reality sandwiches…"

57— Tin-Tan: *See Note 45.*

58— Mariana Larrosa: Mara Larrosa. *See Note 25.*

59— quiúbole: Mexican slang derived from the phrase "¿Qué hubo?" (What was it?), a term equivalent to "What's up?"

60— Pedro Damián Masson (1954-): Poet associated with the infrarealists who wrote a controversial essay, "La carcajada del topo" ("The Cackling Laugh of the Mole"), critical of a number of Mexican establishment poets of the 1970s.

61— José Revueltas: *See Note 7.*

62— In Mezcalina station / Of the Kimosari Metro: There is, of course, no Mezcalina station in the non-existent Kimosari Metro, but Mezcalina obviously refers to mescaline. "Kimosari" has no certain meaning although it may refer to the term "Ke-mo sah-bee" used by Tonto on the American program *The Lone Ranger.*

63— José Guadalupe Posada (1852-1913): Mexican printer and lithographer. He gained fame for his satirical political broadsides that depicted the wealthy and powerful and the poor as skeletons to remind the vain and presumptuous that death awaits everyone.

64— Tepito fingers: Tepito is a very poor barrio in Mexico City, known for crime in the market areas where numerous thieves and pick-pockets rove with what Anglos would call "sticky fingers."

65— kafka: Here, the poet has created a verb out of the surname of Franz Kafka.

66— For Patricia: At the time of publication, this person could not be identified with any certainty. There is a possibility that she is the Patricia Rodríguez Acosta to whom the poem "In the Gateway of the Clouds" is dedicated.

67— Mazateca: Refers to an indigenous people of Mexico whose traditional territories straddle the Sierra Mazateca in the state of Oaxaca. The Mazatecas cultivate psychedelic mushrooms for ritual religious purposes.

68— Gordon Ross: At the time of publication this person could not be identified with any certainty. Possibly refers to R. Gordon Wasson (1898-1986), a U.S. banker and amateur ethnomycologist who undertook expeditions in Mexico to study the use of psychoactive mushrooms among the Mazateca (*See Note 67*). The curandera and shaman María Sabina (*See Note 81*) permitted Wasson to partake in Mazatecan rituals and consume "magic" mushrooms. Wasson's reports of his adventures were widely circulated in the U.S. and sparked interest in the psychedelic fungi.

69— Toltec: A Nahuatl-speaking people of considerable cultural and trade-based influence during the period before the Aztecs occupied the Valley of Mexico.

70— guamúchil: A leguminous tree (*Pithecellobium dulce)* native to Mexico. It produces pods containing a sweet and sour pulp used as an accompaniment to meat dishes or is mixed with water and sugar to make refreshing drinks.

71— King Lopitos: "El Rey Lopitos" was the nickname bestowed on Alfredo López Cisneros (1923-1966), a city councilman and charismatic community leader of the poverty-plagued Acapulco barrio known as "La Laja." López Cisneros was known for his influence and ability to raise small armies of the poor to confront the rich developers of Acapulco. He came into conflict with municipal and state authorities and was assassinated on the street by persons unknown.

72— José Revueltas: *See Note 7.*

73— el Indio Bedoya: This was the sobriquet (meaning "Bedoya the Indian") given to Alfonso Bedoya (1904-1957), a film actor who appeared in nearly 175 Mexican movies and over 40

American films, the most famous of which was *The Treasure of the Sierra Madre*. In that film, Bedoya utters the famous line: "Badges? I don't have to show you any stinking badges!"

74— huizache: A thorny acacia tree (*Vachellia farnesiana*) native to Mexico.

75— San Juan de Letrán: A metro station in Mexico City.

76— Bataclán: A bar and nightclub in Mexico City named for the famous theater and night club in Paris.

77— Monte Albán: Although it is possible that this is a reference to a Zapotec archeological site near Oaxaca, it is more likely a reference to a street by the same name that runs through the barrio of Letrán Valle in Mexico City.

78— Sons of King Lopitos: *See Note 71.*

79— Beltrán Morales (1944-1986): Abrasive Nicaraguan poet and critic who, like Efraín Huerta (*See Note 50*), advocated a colloquial short-lined verse. He is associated by many with anti-poetry, such as the work of Nicanor Parra.

80— Laurels & Hardys: Translation of "Gordos & flacos," a reference to the comedy team of Oliver Hardy and Stan Laurel, popularly called "El gordo y el flaco" (the fat one and the skinny one) throughout Mexico.

81— Marías Sabinas: Refers to María Sabina (1894-1985), a Mazateca curandera (healer or shaman) whose healing techniques centered on the use of psilocybin mushrooms. Sabina was the first known Mazateca shaman to allow white foreigners to partake in traditional ritualistic healing vigils during which psilocybin mushrooms were ingested to commune with ancestral spirits and gods. Her chants were recorded and translated by Henry Munn and published by R. Gordon Wasson.

82— Kyra Galvan (1956-): Mexican, poet, novelist, economist, photographer, translator, and journalist. She attended the poetry workshop at The Casa del Lago Juan José Arreola cultural center. *See Note 83.*

83— Claudia Kerik (1957-): Translator, essayist and professor of Hispanic Letters at the Universidad Autónoma de México (UNAM). Born in Argentina, her family immigrated to Mexico in 1970. In the mid-1970s, she participated in the poetry workshop directed by Alejandro Aura at the Casa del Lago Juan José Arreola, a cultural center located in Chapultepec Park in Mexico City, founded as an extension of UNAM. The infrarealists Roberto Bolaño, Mario Santiago, and Rubén Medina attended this workshop at the same time. Mario Santiago ultimately fell in unrequited love with Kerik, and when she decided to move to Israel in 1977, Mario Santiago pursued her.

84— Mezcalina: Mescaline

85— Now that I have no hope of ever returning again: Translator's rendering of the poet's quotation of Cavalcanti: "Ya que no espero nunca más volver." Cavalcanti's original line is: "Perch'i' no spero di tornar giammai," which the translator would phrase as "Because I have no hope of ever returning."

Mario Santiago Papasquiaro: A Brief Biographical Note

Mario Santiago (1953-1998) was a poet errant, an incessant wanderer of the storied streets of Mexico City and an adventurous pursuer of love in Europe and the Middle East.

In his mid-twenties he met a young woman, Claudia Kerik, at a poetry workshop (attended, also, by Roberto Bolaño and other infrarealists) held in a cultural center in Chapultepec Park. Mario Santiago became infatuated with her. His love was not returned. When Kerik, who was Jewish, decided to emigrate to Israel in 1977, he followed her. He went to Paris and made his way to Jerusalem and worked on a nearby kibbutz to be near her. When he finally gave up his romantic pursuit, he made a slow retreat through Europe, writing poetry whenever he could. In Vienna, he was jailed for participating in a political demonstration and was expelled from Austria. He worked as a dishwasher in Barcelona and a fisherman and crop picker in the south of France, and he was a vagabond in Paris before finally going back to Mexico.

A rebellious man with a prickly personality and anti-social tendencies, he had difficulty holding down a job. He would burn off excess energy by taking long walks, at times for days on end but always coming home to the most important person in his life, his wife Rebeca López, the familial anchor who provided him the love and support necessary to his work. He was injured when hit by a car while on one of his interminable hikes. This did not deter him from taking his long meditative walks, but thereafter he had to use a cane.

After his accident, he became reckless and would cross busy streets with no regard for oncoming traffic, and on January 10, 1998, he was struck by a hit-and-run driver and killed.

After he had been missing several days, his wife called the police. She was directed to a morgue where she identified a corpse as her husband.

Printed in Dunstable, United Kingdom

64667577R00132